DoubleSpeak in Black and White

Part of *The Cultural Literacy Trilogy*, An American Debriefing and A New millennium Discussion

DoubleSpeak in Black and White

America Needs a New Idea, The Worlds First Cultural Poisoning Self-Test.

DoubleSpeak in Black and White will help Americans in general, and African Americans in particular, identify Cultural Poisoning, understand how to cure it, and most importantly, how to prevent your children from catching it.

Rudy Aunk

Writers Club Press

San Jose New York Lincoln Shanghai

DoubleSpeak in Black and White
America Needs a New Idea, The Worlds First Cultural Poisoning Self-Test.

Writers Club Press
an imprint of iUniverse, Inc.

For information address:
iUniverse, Inc.
5220 S. 16th St., Suite 200
Lincoln, NE 68512
www.iuniverse.com

I am not a doctor, and the advise in this book is not intended as medical advice. Some readers could find the information in this book unsittling. The culturally sensitive, should proceed from this point with caution, if at all.
To contact the author:
Email: raunk@iname.com
Web Site: Cultural Literacy Central http://come.to/aunk
Cultural Literacy 101 Club http://forums.delphiforums.com/CLtalk/start

ISBN: 0-595-22858-5

Printed in the United States of America

DEDICATION

To my children and all the youth of the world who are our future. To my spiritual mate who kept my spirit in balance and my person focused.

For it is they who are truly responsible for the assembling of the three technoglyphs (circle, triangle and tree) into the metaphor called the Cultural Literacy Map.

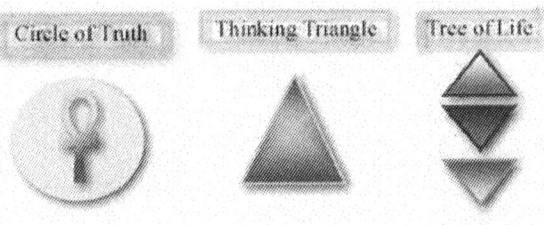

The spiritual pull from my children and my mate produced the drive in me to create the map.

The desire to convey my understanding of my culture to my loved ones is at the base of all my writing. And so I've dedicated my efforts to them.

Classical Afrikan Proverbs[i]

The closer you get to the **truth** the simpler it is.

The blessings of thy eternal part are health, Vigor, and proportion the greatest of these is health. What health is to the body, even that is **honesty** to the soul.

"**Be not fooled,** magic cannot alter the laws of nature, all must be according to Law, but an adept can, through control of thoughts and Law, alter the perception of the spectators since the senses bring information not knowledge"

FIRST THING: TAKE THE TEST

Complete the self-test on the next page

Before You Read the Table of Contents

Before the Preface

Before You Skim

Test Your Self!

The book is based on Your Answers

The first thing you need to do to begin our discussion, is to take the one minute self test on the next page in <u>ink</u>. Please feel free to write in the book.

If you are reading this book as an electronic book, please write your answers in a permanent place. Ie. An electronic sticky note on the test page, on a mobile electronic appliance like a PDA (Personal Data Assistant) or a standard piece of paper.

You will find that this book is different from other traditional books. That is the book is based on the input you provide to yourself through the self test and the discussion we are about to have.

Your original writtten answers will be used for an important self asessment exercise at the end of the book

THE CULTURAL POISONING SELF TEST
AN AMERICAN CULTURAL "DEBRIEFING"

Like the home pregnancy test or the home diabetes test, this is the home cultural test. Are all the things you know **true**? The test will ask you about subjects you are already familiar with. That is **information you know, believe or have formed an opinion about**. It is the interactive part of the process of your debriefing yourself. All the answers are "YES or "NO" except for two of the questions. You should try to answer all questions to the best of your knowledge or recollection. In the rare event that you have no idea or thoughts at all about a possible answer it is ok to write, "I don't know". You will find the answers on the following pages. Like all cultural literacy information, don't take my word or opinion for it; check it out for yourself.

1. Were all the **maps** we learned from in school more or less accurate?
2. How many **continents** are there and is Europe one of them?
3. In what country is **Classical African Civilization** located?
4. Did **Columbus** discover America?
5. Was President **George Washington** a hero to all Americans?
6. Are the popular Western pictures of **Jesus Christ** consistent with his physical description in the Holy Bible?
7. Do you, a member of your family, or a friend of yours have **good hair?** (That is, would you agree that straight or curly hair is more desirable than "kinky" hair)?
8. Is the **divorce rate** 50% or higher all over the world?
9. Is everyone at high risk of getting **skin cancer** from staying in the sun?
10. Does it make any difference what color your **family doctor** is?

CONTENTS

PREFACE

America is still infected by racism and needs a new idea, if it is to finally reach its constitutional ideal of life, liberty, and the pursuit of happiness for all its citizens. This opening sentence is the premise upon which this book is based.

On one level this book is about **language and culture**. On another level it contains information that African Americans in particular and Americans in general will find indispensable, as they think about their future in the new millennium.

This book *Doublespeak In Black And White, America needs a new idea* is one of the first products of a new project, called the Cultural Literacy Project (CLP) It is **intended to provide a new analysis** of America's "race" Problem. This contemporary analysis is what we refer to as a new idea for America. *Doublespeak In Black And White* will introduce you to a number of new ideas and alert you to additional ideas you should become familiar with (covered in future CLP works). Specifically, I will be introducing you to the cultural literacy project and providing you with a test, which is the main feature of this book, that will assist you in gaining a clearer understanding of your attitudes regarding your own ethnic group and other ethnic groups.

As we move toward the next century, we **need to stop and take stock** of what we have learned from the past, and what we know and believe about the present. Truthful information from the past and present should serve as a **compass guiding us into the future**.

My name is Rudy Aunk. You will note that my name is a composite of my American name and my African name and therefore you should rightly conclude that I am an African American. As I am unwilling to divorce myself from either the American or African parts of my being, I will not be providing you with a purely American analysis as some have urged me to do. Nor will I be providing a purely African analysis as others have urged me too. The information regarding America's race problem while from an African American perspective; is for all Americans.

One of the main reasons for the Cultural Literacy Project is **President Clinton's national discussion** on "race". While this is a timely and necessary national priority it is prone to the **start up problems** of any project. For instance initially Native Americans were not invited to the discussion table. This has since been corrected. There are at least two other problems that the National Discussion faces with which the CLP can be of help. One, Americans are coming to the discussion table **unprepared** and two, there is no clear **language** for discussing the American "race" problem.

By unprepared I mean some individuals are just showing up at the table without taking the time to get up to speed on the historical perspectives of the other members of the discussion. The other and more important problem is that there is **no existing language** to discuss the problems of "race" in America. That is, there are literally no words to describe some of the thoughts regarding "race" that must be discussed. For example how do you have an effective discussion on "race" when every one at the table has a different definition for the words "race" and "ethnicity"? The CLP, including this book, intends to add information to the discussion which will enable an individual to come to the table better prepared and provide a new set of words intended to begin to address the inherent "race" language problems. I should note at this point that this language problem is not just an inter-ethnic group problem. It is also an intra-ethnic group problem. For example, in the African American ethnic group, there are in many instances common feelings regarding America's "race" problem however, there is no common language to effectively and efficiently express those feelings and/or facts.

An example of what I mean can be found in my simple **observations of African American discussions** on "race" over the years. There is a recurring

1,2,3 pattern to these discussions. (1) **The opening**: the participants seem to disagree on a "race" issue or set of issues. (2) **The middle game**: they spend 50% or more of their time defining terms, that is figuring out what each other really means by what they are saying. (3) **The end game**: they conclude that they were really in agreement all the time and just using different words to describe the same thing or set of thoughts. Or as is often the case, they'll conclude that they in fact disagree. Regardless of which of these two end game scenarios is the case, the one consistent thing about them is that they do not result in a solution. In the end the parties to these "race" game discussions tend to feel that despite the fact that they may have learned something, they have been around a familiar circle with no real solution in sight. The conclusions I reached from my observations are that the language used to discuss "race" is very inefficient and sometimes actually counter productive.

By **counter productive language** I mean that conversations on "race" often end because the participants can't agree on terms or strongly object to the terms used by the other participants. The same 1,2,3 patterns can be observed in the National discussion on "race".

Any discussion where the participants spend 50% of their time "defining terms" is going to be ineffective. **Imagine if doctors**, every time they met, spent 50% of their time defining the terms they would use to describe the heart when trying to resolve some medical problem. Many medical problems would remain unresolved simply because of the **inefficiency of the medical language**.

The **medical profession** overcomes their potential language inefficiency problem by having a common very well defined medical vocabulary. There are medical dictionaries and even schools for medical secretaries to learn the common language. Another place where **inefficient communication is minimized** is in corporate Americas **sales organizations** like IBM and Microsoft. Every sales person in describing a sales situation or sales problem can tell you whether they are in the presenting, clarifying or closing stage of the sale. Corporations spend millions on sales communication training because they need sales men to spend the least amount of time talking to each other about sales situations and most of their time selling.

The language used to discuss America's "race" problem may never reach the level of language efficiency achieved by the medical profession, but it is essential that it at least reach the language efficiency levels of corporate salesmen.

The conclusion is obvious. If we could **raise the language efficiency in the national discussion on "race"** more "race" related problems could be resolved. Said another way; efficient "race" language can aid problem resolution in the same way that efficient medical language enables problem resolution in any medical discussion.

What **we have been talking about is language mechanics.** That is the psychological use of language (words) to contract or expand the range of human thought. The study of language used for good or for evil is not new. Classical Africans were aware of the power of misrepresenting reality. See the *Don't Be Fooled* Proverb at the beginning of the book. George Orwell in his classic book *1984* demonstrated and predicted the psychological use of language for mass population control. "Big Brother" was very effective at using language to control the range of thought of its country's citizens. Professor William Lutz, the modern Orwell, in his series of books on the subject of **"Doublespeak"** has delineated how corrupt language in politics has been the cause of inefficiency and counter productivity in the government. Countless other authors have written books on **reverse psychology** and language.

So the study of language as a psychological tool for good and evil is not a new idea. Taking this established body of knowledge and applying its lessons to the American "race" problem is a new idea for America.

*　　　　　　*　　　　　　*

The main idea that I am trying to convey to you in this preface is that language is a key tool, indispensable to resolving America's "race" problem.

There is a specialized language that can be utilized. The flow chart below will help pinpoint what I mean.

I mentioned professor Lutz's Doublespeak work. In the flow chart the

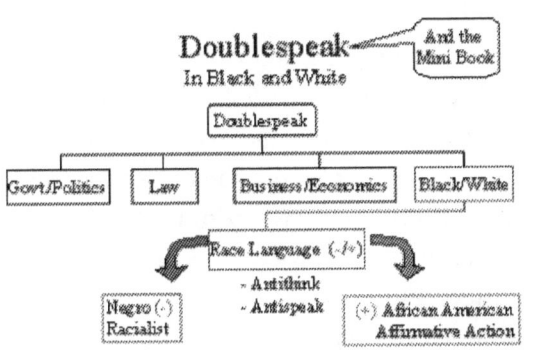

first three boxes under doublespeak represents the specialized areas of language that Professor Lutz focuses on. The fourth box **"Black/White"** is a new area of specialized language that the cultural literacy strategy, which you will learn about, is focused on.

Doublespeak words **mis-represent reality**. Race language has positive and negative words. That is words that represent reality and words that do not. The negative words are the ones that cause confusion in American communication on America's "race" problem. Our objective is the simple eliminating, redefining or the constructing of common clear definitions for negative "race" words. This will reduce communication fuzziness regarding "race". Let me give you a few of professor Lutz's examples to give you a feel for how this works. "Doublespeak turns lies told by politicians into 'strategic misrepresentations,' 'reality augmentation', or 'terminological inexactitudes'." This is called putting a spin on things (confusing reality). Lutz points out that if we are going to fix politics we must start with political language. So again, the cultural literacy project asserts that if we are going to fix America's "race" problem we must start with "race" language.

Let us take a look at **an example** of how this new tool might work to reduce the counter productive aspects of race language and improve the efficiency of "race" language. For instance, could we have a discussion on the history and current status of America's "race" problem that is substantially more efficient and effective by defining just three terms up front? Let's give it a shot.

The following brief **discussion regarding racism and anti-humanism** will give you a feel for how this information process will work regarding improving an individual's preparedness for the national discussion on "race" and utilizing new language tools to make the discussion more efficient. The first thing we will do is clarify the definition of two commonly used words, racism and racist and add a new term, anti-humanist. These changes will constitute our three—term experiment.

I understand that you may not agree with the following definitions provided for racism and racist. However, I am asking you to bear with me for the sake of this experiment and at least temporarily program your bio-computer with these definitions.

*   *   *

For the sake of this discussion we will use the following **three simplified definitions**:

Racism: The local/Global system of White supremacy.

Racist: An individual who subscribes to the tenants of White supremacy.

Anti-humanist: An American who is in favor of life liberty and the pursuit of happiness for some.

Now that we have defined our terms we need to set the **parameters of the discussion**. The discussion will be in two parts, the history of America's "race" problem and the status of the problem. We must be able to complete this ordinarily complex and lengthy discussion in approximately two pages (two minutes). With our terms defined let's get started with our example/experiment.

Historically the "race" problem goes back a long way. For the sake of our discussion since we are in America lets start at an obvious, common point. Since the creation of the United States of America, the American "race" problem has existed. **Racism in America has not ended** it has just changed it's form, from overt to covert. This being the case, it then follows that it is not yet time for Americans of good will to end their fight against America's "race" problem. It is time for Americans to amend their fight against the forces of evil in America.

All Americans, especially European Americans must come to grips with the fundamental reality that racism is historically a fundamental value of American society. That is to say, **racism is a fundamental value of American society** in the same sense that rugged individualism is a core American value.

Most African Americans and Native Americans have always been unconsciously aware of this fact of life. Despite the fact that many books have been written on the subject from non-fiction to fiction and poetry, most **Americans have** not **yet internalized this reality**. They have neither consciously, nor formally acknowledged it.

It was not historically the case, as is believed by many, that a "few European Americans" were "racists"(White supremacists). The facts are that **most European Americans were racists** from the founding "fathers" to the individual plantation owners who could not read, to the common citizen. This fundamental American racism value was (some will say still is) a major part of the American individual value system. It was **a major**

American family value, a major governmental value, and it was built into most American institutions as a fundamental value.

Now I have just said some things that **many readers will immediately object** to as being too strong or simply untrue. They will say, "Come on, racism was not a fundamental American family value." To those who jump to that conclusion, I would ask how racism gets passed from one human being to another in the first place, if not from parent to child? More racism has been **taught at American family dinner tables** than at any Klan rally. It's just that the majority of those people don't tend to graduate from the dinner table to the Klan meeting except, in the most extreme cases. Most readers have seen (or should have seen) one of **the pictures of African Americans being hanged in Old America.** They typically show an African American hanging from a tree, with a whole town of European Americans, and their children standing around watching the festivities. Now I ask you in that example were the children teaching the parents racism or was it the other way around? And that is just one of many examples from American history. Stop and really think about this for a minute. If your "father" was a racist, there is a higher probability that you will be a racist or prejudiced, than if your father and/or mother was not a racist.[ii]

Don't kid yourself, this basic American family value **has not disappeared it has just changed it's modes** of expression. That is why we are having this national discussion on "race"!

A conservative, republican 1996 presidential candidate, Bob Dole created a slogan **"Building a Bridge to the Past"**. This slogan was intended to remind Americans that what we need to do is return to our old American family values. Now, a lot of Americans thought this was a good idea. Obviously Native Americans and African Americans would not like to return to the values of the past considering the family value of racism. The good news is most Americans rejected this slogan and the republicans eventually dropped it. The slogan that prevailed in the 96 election was

"**Building a bridge to the future**". This is an indication that most Americans are at least headed in the right general direction.

Now naturally the **family is not the only source** for becoming infected by racism. However, it is the place where most Americans are either inoculated against racism, or gain a proclivity toward it.

If you have not previously thought about this potential parental impact on your attitude toward other ethnic groups, you may want to give it some more thought. A good place to start might be to give yourself the **Parental Influence Test**.[iii] That is, ask yourself the question " **were my parents racists or prejudiced?**" You may not be exactly clear about your own attitudes toward other ethnic groups but, your memory of your parents' (or other parental figures) attitudes regarding other ethnic groups may give you some insight into your acquired attitudes (however subconscious).

Racism as a historical American individual and group reality is an **attitude that hardened into a belief system**. This belief system became part of the law of the land, from the constitution to the separate but equal laws.

Over time **racism in America has degenerated into a general attitude of anti-humanism**. By anti-humanism I mean the attitude of disenfranchising various American ethnic groups by depriving them of their civil rights and/or human rights. Said another way, the bad attitude about African Americans, and Native Americans, and the behavior of disenfranchising them mutated into the larger codified practice of disenfranchising many other American groups. If you doubt that this mutation took place, all you have to do is read the writings of early American Women, Asians, Irish, Italians, Jews, Mexicans, Puerto Ricans etc. These groups all testify to varying levels of hate, discrimination, prejudice and disenfranchisement being visited upon their human group by the majority American group. The historic reality of these groups, although not as intense or long lasting as the attacks on African Americans, or Native Americans, marked the transition of the American "race" problem from only a Black /White conflict or, even Brown/White conflict into something much broader.

Anti-humanism is the moral and practical material that America's "race" problem is made of. As America has always had anti-humanists, she has also had humanists who have lead the fight to mitigate America's "race" problem. The most recent battle in this fight has been the civil rights battle, which is still in progress. Unfortunately America's forward momentum in dealing with her "race" problem has stalled after the great progress of the 1960's.

There are two reasons for the momentum stall in the progress on America's "race" problem. First, America has put the subject of racism in **the national closet.** Second, **anti-humanists have gone underground.** Overt racism was participated in or tolerated in old America. Overt racism is no longer tolerated in contemporary America. So the racists and anti-humanists are harder to identify as they are typically hiding behind public politically correct behavior. This national conversion from overt racism to covert racism has temporarily disoriented humanists. Friend and foe could have easily been identified by the old rules of the race game however, that is not the case today.

Bull Conner of the 60's, with his dogs and water hoses was a clear anti-humanist. **His modern counter parts** hidden behind politically correct rhetoric, and behaviors have adapted a kind of stealth quality that enables them to **slip by the humanist radar.** Therefore humanists must develop a new analysis of the situation on the ground and formulate a new battle plan to address the new realities of the "race" game.

At the end of our example/experiment we find that **small adjustments in language** (three words) can create quantum leaps in the efficiency of race language. It is this new bottom line type of clarity that is needed in the National discussion on "race". A change in language can produce the needed clarity that can increase the probability that the National discussion will actually produce some useful results.

As we come to the end of the preface let's summarize what we have discussed. **America is still infected** by racism and needs a new idea. I am writing from an African American perspective but the information is for all Americans. The National discussion is a good thing that has some predictable and identifiable start up problems. Language efficiency is the key to getting past the start up problems.

We need to apply existing lessons regarding the **impact of language on human psychology** as it pertains to the "race" problem. We gave you an example of how clarifying a few words can improve language efficiency. The example also provided some basic information about the history and status of America's "race" problem. Basic information you will need to be prepared for the National discussion, and to understand the information in this book.

ACKNOWLEDGEMENTS

Many people have helped shape the information presented for discussion in The Cultural Literacy Trilogy and in this book. There are far too many to list here. First thank you to the African American Culturally Literate community and all the elders and scholars whose wisdom and resurrection of African classical culture have freed my spirit. Charles, my life long friend, who started me on this path despite myself. Ra Un Nefer Amen, author of Metu Neter the first modern human to comprehensively describe for the public the thinking and wisdom of the ancient Kamitans (Egyptians). Imhotep who through his radio program introduced me to Dr. Ben, Dr. Clark, Dr. Van Sertima and so many of our great scholars. Carol Barns for his great research and information on melanin. Those who I have not mentioned you know who you are and thank you very much.

Acknowledgment is also made to the following publishers and authors for permission to use copyrighted material:

Friendship Press New York, New York. Peters Projection. For information contact Friendship Press, 474 Riverside Drive (772) New York, NY 10115

Carol Barns, Houston, Texas. Author of Melanin: Chemical key to Black greatness and Jazzy Melanin. Contact Carol Barns P.O. Box 300918 Houston, Texas 77230-0918

INTRODUCTION

DoubleSpeak was first published just before the turn of the millenium in 1998 as an E-Book. This is the first traditional earth bound version and revised E-book. This information is much the same as the 98 version but, I have organized it a little better then my first attempt and corrected some errors. I am confident that the new structure will make it easier for readers to find things and use the book as a standard reference for Cultural Poisoning.

The new structure is simple I have divided the book into three parts Cultural Poisoning, Cultural Literacy, and "Race" in the Third Millenium. In the introduction, I will describe what is in each section, do some defining of terms house keeping, and then we will be off to the main body of the book.

Hopefully, the very first thing you did when you opened this book was to **take the Cultural Poisoning Self -Test.** (If you did not take the test please do so now!). This test enables you to think about and record your ideas regarding culture. Most of what we do in part one depends on the way you recorded your cultural thoughts in the beginning of the book.

The following summarizes the book's structure:

In the Preface I point out that unlike many other millenium analysis of the American "Race" Problem, we conclude that language is a major part of the problem and at the base of the solution.

In Part I Cultural Poisoning (CP): You are introduced to the Cultural Literacy Project. As you learn about the project you will be learning new words, and phrases that are essential to getting the fullest understanding of the answers to the Cultural Poisoning Test. The balance of Part I is devoted to providing you with the answers to the CP Test. At the end of Part I we raise some questions that go beyond the test.

In Part II Cultural Literacy: Cultural Literacy Minutes are explained and used to inform you of the ramifications of CP beyond your local area regarding inter-ethnic relations. You will be introduced to Classical African Civilization through one of its best know symbols the Aunk.

In Part III "Race" In the New Millenium: We set a clear and compelling objective for the new millenium, and introduce you to the Action Plan necessary to achieve the objective.

Ok that covers the basic structure of the book, now on to the house keeping items.

The Cultural Literacy Project (CLP) of which this book is a part was created among other things to make the point **"don't end the fight, amend the fight.** The project therefore proposes a new idea regarding the amendment of the fight to resolve America's "race" problem. The CLP calls this strategic adjustment "The Cultural Literacy Strategy". The strategy proposes as its main weapons Language and Cultural Literacy. *Doublespeak In Black And White* will start to bring the reader up to speed on these new weapons.

The main feature of the book is the Cultural Literacy Self Test. The **ten questions** are asked and the direct answer to each question is provided. And the Bigger Questions behind the basic questions are also raised briefly. Melanin is the only "Bigger Question" subject that I have given extended treatment because of its importance to the process of thought I am asking you to engage in.

The format of this book is intentionally a fast paced short page-turner. The **short format and low cost** makes the basic information available to the widest possible audience. It is also an easy book to give to someone you think will benefit from joining our discussion. **Maybe someone gave you the book**. If so, this is an opportunity to join a discussion, and thought process you might have otherwise missed. When opportunity knocks it is a wise person who opens the door. No matter how you got the book you are about to start a journey to the future. So lets get started and remember this book is **mainly intended to cause you to think**. That is think about yourself, and your ethnic group(s). Any improvement in America's interethnic behavior starts with you.

Now we need to take care of some **basic house keeping** items. The items are a commentary on footnote use and defining some terms that are not defined elsewhere in the book. These items are really **more for the academic community** and some **special interest groups** that have raised particular questions with me during my research. The general reader will most likely see this as unnecessary hair splitting and **may wish to skip this section**. To skip this, just go down to defining terms.

The foot note crutch: a footnote in the West tends to be a thinking crutch. That is to say Westerners tend to use the presence of a footnote to avoid critically thinking about information presented to them. I have purposely minimized the use of footnotes in this book because, I am asking you to use your critical thinking skills. Most of the information in this book simply requires that you use your logic, and common sense to reach conclusions about the information presented. Naturally, certain types of footnoting are appropriate and even necessary. As in the case of technical information from others that the reader may want to learn more about. To that end a combined notes-bibliography section is also provided at the end of this book.

In Classical African Civilization sources were sometimes used. Footnoting was generally not used. The inventors of writing oddly enough applied a different standard to classical authors then we apply to writers today. They expected the veracity of a work to stand or fall of its own merit. For those to whom western education makes this notion of the writer/reader relationship foreign, I ask you to try it. You might like it. Bear with me, critically think about the information presented.

Try to **avoid going down the Greek road** (Western) of wanting to kill Socrates for "corrupting the minds of the youth, by teaching foreign doctrines". The information is new and may seem foreign to many. However, despite your perception of some of the rhetoric, the intent is to provide new ideas that will improve the quality of life for all Americans. Try to avoid the western left brain propensity to expend excess amounts of energy on Western literary details, at the expanse of failing to critically think about the important points raised.

For those individuals who will have a propensity to throw up rhetorical **cultural straw men** to attack or otherwise besmirch the work of the project based on footnote foolishness (its not true unless it has a footnote), understand that we will not suffer fools. On the other hand **if I made an error** (not only possible, but also quite likely) and failed to include a footnote that you need to reach an important conclusion, please email me at raunk@iname.com and I will make every effort to provide you with the appropriate source.

*   *   *

Defining Terms:

Most of the terms that you will need to understand the new concepts contained in this book will be explained in the section of the book called the " Cultural Literacy Project Overview". I have listed some of the important exceptions below.

African and Afrikan: the use of the letter "K" **in the word Africa is not a spelling error.** There are **two very different views of Africa**, which must be distinguished. European Americans and other Americans who see things through European glasses[1] have one view of Africa. Culturally literate African Americans have a much different view. The **European American view** (thoughts / images) of Africa is that of a dark jungle filled with exotic animals and superstitious native savages. They see their interaction with Africans as a mixed bag, Some bad "slavery" and some good. They would like to think that Europeans brought civilization to Africans. The **Culturally literate view** is similar to the following. Afrika is the original land of plenty, with the greatest variety of animals, minerals, flora and fauna. It is the home of the original human beings and the creators of civilization. And from classical times to today Africa contains some of the most spiritually advanced people on the planet.

It is my judgement that the two images of the same place are so drastically different, that it requires a literary device for distinguishing the two views. So I have adapted the "K" convention used by many Afrikan writers in the African American community. I realize that switching between the king's English spelling **Africa/African and Afrika/Afrikan** spelling may be confusing to those who are new to the concept, so I have used it sparingly in this book. However it is important that you be familiar with the concept, and the thinking that it represents. It is part of becoming culturally literate.

White and Caucasian: My research has indicated that I need to clarify my use of these terms for some of my readers. For instance, conservative members of the African American community have advised me that I should not use the word "White" to represent Caucasians as the word does not represent reality. That is individuals who are called White are in reality more pink or off white visually. They assert that the use of the word White is psychologically damaging. I hear your argument and without

---

[1] Read almost any European history book discussing Africa from the 1600's to the 1960's to get a view of Africa through European glasses (view/perspective).

going into the details of the conservative analysis which has some cultural merit, not using the word White is impractical in my judgement. Given the state of the National discussion on "race" it would in fact be counter-productive. Let me assure my conservative brothers that I understand the difference between symbolic ethnic words like White, Red, Yellow and Black as opposed to using biological, geographical ethnic words like Caucasian, Native American, Asian and African.

Having said that let me tell you **how I will be using the words** in the context of this book. I will use the symbolic terms Black and White to draw a contrast or comparison. I will use the geographic, and ethnic, descriptive words African, Asian and Caucasian as image composite words that both describe the biological, and cultural ethnicity, of a group and their geographical origin.

As you read this book or any other book, understand that use of the words Black and White are not subject to stop being used anytime soon. And knowing that both words have positive and negative stereotypical baggage attached to them, depending on the cultural viewpoint of individuals it is important to actively start to deprogram your bio-computer every time you see the words Black and White. Deprogramming is achieved by consciously deleting the negative stereotype from your bio-computer whenever they pop up on your mental screen.

America needs a common definition of the words Black and White. The word Black comes in to language at the dawn of recorded history. The word White comes into recorded history much later, however, it has been used in America for a long time. In my considered opinion it is not the case that these words should not be used. In fact their short conciseness makes them very effective language tools. The cultural challenge for Americans is coming to a common reality based popular definition of the terms. The information presented in this book, among other things, is intended to assist Americans move toward new common definitions of the terms Black and White.

A final word, on the **use of the word Caucasian** as an image composite word which some may find problematic. It is true that scientists are not in unanimous agreement regarding a geographic location for the origin of White people on the earth. And certainly, there is considerable discussion and divergence of opinion regarding this issue in the African American community. However, there is significant scientific evidence that indicates, the earliest geographic location where substantial populations of human beings with melanin levels consistent with White people was located. This location as far as I have been able to understand is the area of southwest Asia around the Caucasus Mountains. So, as a practical matter of competitive plausibility and popular familiarity, I will use the designation Caucasian as an image composite word until, such time as new more unanimous scientific evidence either confirms this hypothesis, or overturns it.

Race: Another area where certain groups have expressed concern is with **our use of the word "race"**. They typically assert that "race" is a culturally poisoned term itself and we should not use it. First let me say that the cultural literacy project agrees with those who have raised this issue. That is why you see the word "race" in quotes. The Project does its part to point out that there is one "race" the human race, with many ethnic groups. Biologists classify the one human race as genus *Homo*, and species *sapiens*.[iv]

*   *   *

There are **two things that I won't be doing**: using the term Black racist or engaging in one brush syndrome. I would like to clarify the meanings of both of these terms.

There are Blacks who don't like or distrust Whites with cause. There are Europhobic Blacks. There are even a few psychopathically disturbed African Americans who might do harm to European Americans with out cause. These Blacks might be called many things, but not "Black racists".

There is no Black equivalent to a White racist. When Blacks have killed tens of millions of Europeans and amassed vast national wealth by stealing free European American labor, then someone might be justified in making some reality-based comparison. Until that time, all such references are ludicrous. There is only one type of racist, the historic definition that all Americans should know, the White supremacist. Don't believe the hype. "Black racist" is a doublespeak non-reality term.

One Brush Syndrome: It is important to note that **painting any ethnic group blindly with the same stereotypical paintbrush is an error.** For those, African Americans who are inclined to think that all Whites are bad, I would remind you that their were European American stops on the underground railroad. For anyone who is critically thinking it should be clear that I am always making a distinction for instance between the historic White group, the contemporary White group, and the individual European American whom I may be speaking to today, one on one. As Dr. Martin Luther King said, a person should be judged by the content of their character. That is what you can see of their character from their language, and from their behavior.

In modern times we see President Clinton, on the continent of Africa, saying that Europeans were wrong to enslave Africans. For the first time in American history the Country's President has not only called for a national discussion on "race", but is taking the risk of participating in the discussions himself. The contents of this book are directed toward individuals of the president's ilk, from all ethnic groups, who have demonstrated humanistic tendencies.

*   *   *

A final word on the test you have just taken.

The self-test may seem to be a group of random questions. Let me assure you that they are not. The questions are carefully selected and do fit a pattern.

Each of the questions was chosen for a specific reason, and fits into three categories of detection/correction.

THE QUESTION MAP

Geographic Cultural Orientation
Personal and Group philosophy
Western Worldview Orientation

The structure of the test is discussed in more detail at the end of the book.

Having completed our house keeping, we have completed the preface. So let's move on to Part I Cultural Poisoning.

PART I

CULTURAL POISONING

THE CULTURAL LITERACY PROJECT
OVERVIEW

Despite considerable progress in America, there are still two America's one Black and one White.[v] Therefore, as the graphic below points out, **America needs a new idea** for the new millennium. By a new **idea I mean a new strategy** for resolving the "race" problem in America. **By strategy I mean**, a new **Action Plan** that incorporates a new way of thinking and behaving by Americans in attempting to address their "race" problems in America.

Before we get into our explanation of the project let me take a minute to **explain some of the assumptions upon which** the Cultural Literacy Project (CLP) is based. If you have been following President Clinton's National

Discussion on Race, you are already familiar with some of the assumptions. **The first assumption** is that Americans are **tired of carrying the**

moral baggage that the "race" problem represents and would like to resolve the problem once and for all.

In addition to the **moral challenges** that the "race" problem represents there is an increasingly prominent set of **practical challenges** inherent in the problem.

The second assumption is that **America wants to be a leadership player in the immerging global village**. However, the rules for geopolitical citizenship have rapidly changed since the days of the Old World Order and the superpowers. The old enemy, the Soviet Union is gone. Japan and other nations are more morally, economically and geo-politically independent then they were under the rules of Old World Order. The rise of technology i.e. worldwide television by satellite and the "Internet" make national and international information more difficult to control. Other countries have Atomic and biological weapons changing the rules of what a "superpower" can and can not accomplish militarily.

Third assumption, America understands that the rules are changing and she needs to reengineer herself, in order to adjust to the new global competition rules and internal cultural realities. Japan has fielded a harmonious national team that has been very effective in the new global competition. European nations are fielding a new team (European common market). These new national teams will be competing in whole new emerging global markets (like China, the Pacific Rim, Latin America, Africa, etc.)

Fourth assumption, globalization events dictate that **America also needs to field a new harmonious National Team**, to be an effective player in the global economic game. Because of this need, **America has a new incentive** to look for and listen to new ideas that have the potential to improve harmony on Team America.

The fifth assumption is that **past and present strategies are insufficient** to produce the kind of national harmony needed to field a globally effective Home Team. From the "war on poverty" to the civil rights strategies fought on the legal, political and economic fronts, none have produced the kind of American harmony needed for America to be effective in a now shrinking multi-ethnic world. The total absence of a clear domestic multi-ethnic policy prevents America from adjusting to the changing cultural demographics in its own back yard.

The **proof that these strategies have not solved the problem** lies in the fact that, while these strategies have helped and are helping to improve the quality of life for all Americans, it **is still necessary to employ them today.** Today the legal battle employ's the "No Justice No Peace" strategy of Rev. Al Sharpton. In politics Rev. Jessie Jackson captured national attention employing the "Rainbow Coalition Strategy". On the economic front we see the rise of the "Black middle class" (affirmative action strategy) and the "new economic strategies" of Black Republicans like Tony Brown. Other American ethnic groups like Native Americans and Latino Americans have been fighting similar battles.

For all the humanist strategies there have always been counter **anti-humanist strategies** in America. So to day we see a range of anti-harmony strategies from **proposition 209** in California (anti affirmative action with no alternate plan) to a pattern of **church burnings** around America. And continuing Police brutality and profiling.

Sixth assumption: we must create a more effective means of shedding light on anti-humanists who actively work against forming an effective Team America.

Let me summarize the assumptions we have discussed up to this point.

1. America is **tired of carrying the "race" problems moral baggage** and would like to resolve it.

2. America would like to be an effective **player in the global village.**

3. America understands that **the geopolitical rules have changed.**

4. **America has a new incentive** to deal with the "race" problem because of it's Team America needs.

5. **Past and present strategies will not fully resolve the problem** and enable a Team America.

6. **More effective light needed for active anti-humanists** working against Team America.

When we look **on the ground to sanity check our assumptions** we note from listening to the national discussion on race, that President Clinton and many others are working from a similar set of assumptions.

The national discussion on race is the first "official recognition" on the part of the government that America still has a serious "race" problem. And that if this problem is not corrected it will erode the quality of life in America, and prevent the harmony essential to a globally competitive Team America.

President Clinton to his credit has listened to the large body of American humanists and **implemented a new strategy** to begin to address America's "race" problem. He has come to realize that while he may not have a solution in hand, the "race" problem can not be solved as long as it is hidden in America's moral closet. As this is not just a moral problem but a practical one for America the president, as a practical leader has devised **a national discussion strategy** to bring the problem out of the closet, and onto the national discussion table.

The President's initiative makes the "race" problem "official" and **leads us to some conclusions** about our assumptions.

It is, or should be obvious looking back on history with 20/20 hindsight regarding the various strategies, that while critical to progress, **none of the strategies standing alone have or will solve the race problem** in America. As in the past they will all help advance Americans toward the goal line and may even score some touch downs; but they will not bring the game to an end.

As we come to the close of the current millenium and **review the successes and failures of the past**, it should be clear that we need a new game plan, a new idea to bring the American "race" game to an end.

Most of American leadership is, or should be aware that **America needs a new Game Plan!** However, the humanists have been less effective at getting this message out. You would think that the national and international issues we have been talking about should make the Team America strategy a top priority and a continuing front-page story in America.

Unfortunately, as I write the Team America strategy is not gaining the traction it needs in America. Anti-humanists have successfully knocked the Team America story off the front pages of American news, and supplanted that national priority with a **presidential penis envy** priority (Clinton/Lewinsky "sex scandal") This is the height of National foolishness. It is a low blow to America in more ways than one.

While there is some levity in the Presidential Penis Envy Strategy of the anti-humanist, I brought up the issue **to make a serious point**. Anti-humanists are alive and well in America. **Do not underestimate** or minimize the impact of **the forces of anti-humanism** on the quality of your life, they are capable of extraordinary feats. As demonstrated by their capacity to supplant the National discussion on "race" with a National discussion on "sex". Their spin-doctors and strategists employ psycho-graphically astute sophisticated new tricknology to achieve their ends. Anti-humanists can usually be found holding the low moral ground. However their new **psychological sex game represents a new low**. It is transparently intended to keep the eyes of dull American minds off the prize. **Don't believe the hype!** Humanists need to wake up, rise up, and put Team America back on the National front burner.

As we conclude the assumptions portion of our discussion let me restate our starting point. At the end of the 20th century there are still two nations, one Black and one White. This fact points out that, we "adults" have failed to solve the problem of, "race" in America, in the last 2 milleniums of the Common Era. The fact of the two America's cries out to us at minimum, to **provide our youth with the tools** to finally resolve the problem of "race" in the third millennium C.E.

With our youth in mind, **the CLP proposes, for your consideration, a fresh analysis** and diagnosis of the problem and a new prescription and a hopeful prognosis for the future. It is a plan of action that does not require an external leader. Once an individual is provided with a framework for personal action, you can lead yourself. That is, lead yourself based on a newly re-calibrated moral compass.

The president's new idea calls for national talk. While **talk is important as a start, action is necessary** to make a difference. The cultural literacy **project's mission is to add action** to the important national discussion in progress.

Now that you are familiar with the assumptions the project has taken into consideration, we can **begin our explanation of the project.** Having introduced you to the issues the question becomes "what is the final solution for America's "race" problem? We purposely us the words "final solution" because we are not trying to simply describe another piece of the puzzle like ethnic group Political, or Economic effectiveness. It is our intent to describe what created the problem, and then put the entire puzzle back together again.

In the balance of the introduction we will summarize the projects proposed new idea, the cultural literacy strategy by answering three questions. **What's the problem? What is the fix? What's in it for you?** You, meaning you, your family, your group and our Nation.

The CL strategy has two main components. The first component is a problem analysis model. The second component is a strategy model. .

I. PROBLEM ANALYSIS MODEL

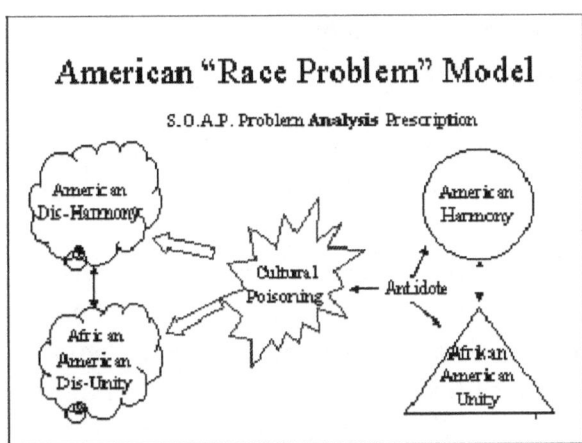

To describe **the project's new analysis** of the "race" problem in America, we have constructed a six-element model. We call this model **The American "Race Problem" Model**. The model gives a summarized view of our analysis and basic prescription (recommended action) to cure the problem.

To analyze America's intractable race problem, a tried and true problem analysis tool was employed that goes by the acronym **S.O.A.P.** Doctors use this problem analysis model to diagnose medical problems. SOAP stands for Subjective, Objective, Analysis and Plan. The Acronym describes the thinking process doctors in a hospital emergency room for instance, utilize to think about life and death situations. Often the doctor may write each element of thinking in a different color in the patient's chart. This enables anyone to quickly determine and review his or her thoughts, at any stage in the standard thinking process used to reach the doctor's conclusions and actions.

Doctors use this standard model for the same **reason most models are used**. Models tend **to reduce confusion** associated with thinking about a new problem or set of circumstances. Using a standard model in addition to aiding the thinking process tends to **reduce the potential for errors** in thinking. They also **provide a standard format for comparing** one doctor's thinking (diagnosis), with other doctors who have had to think about the same problem or set of circumstances (symptoms).

Let's look at an example of the medical model in action to give you a feel for how the SOAP model works as a practical matter.

A doctor in a **hospital emergency room** sees a patient come in. His **subjective** impression (first impression) is that the person is female, in pain and her right arm seems to have a problem. His **objective** diagnosis (After examining the patient) is that she has acute stomach pain and a broken right arm.

His **analysis** after talking to the woman and her family is that. She was in the kitchen intending to drink a glass of water. She was washing clothes at the same time and drank a glass of bleach instead and was poisoned. She panicked and fell down, and broke her right arm. Based on his diagnosis and analysis, his **plan** is to pump her stomach, give her an antidote for the poison, splint the arm and see her in two weeks.

Subjective impressions of America's race problem are more complex than the simple single person emergency room example. Obviously there are more people involved. However we can break all the people into **three basic groups. The no problem group**, that is those who are doing ok and think the problem is fixed ("racism is dead") and the playing field is more or less even. **The Problem can't be fixed group**, that is the problem is worse than ever, intractable and there is no solution in sight. **The problem can be fixed group**, those who feel progress has been made but more work is needed to solve the problem. The members of this last and largest of the groups **fall into two categories.** Those who have a complaint and a solution, and those who just have a complaint. **Those with a complaint** usually have some number of general complaints, i.e. European Americans are evil, "Black on Black crime", racism etc. they do not have a comprehensive definition of the problem and therefore propose no realistic solution. **The other category, (with both a complaint and a solution)** typically have specific complaints and point solutions. They see lack of "education" as the main problem, and therefore believe that education is the total or most of the solution. Others see politics or economics (jobs/money) as the problem, and therefore propose a quick economic fix related to the perceived problem as the ultimate or main solution.

All these **limited impressions are problematic.** Non proposes a comprehensive diagnosis or definition of the problem. Educational effectiveness will certainly help, but is not a total solution. Political or economic effectiveness will help, but is not a total solution. Lack of educational or political effectiveness is part of the problem, but not the total cause of the problem and therefore not the total fix. These quick fixes are proposed because of a lack of understanding of the big picture associated with America's "race" problem.

The general impression that **the race problem is primarily or totally a Black problem** that Blacks should fix is a wrong perception. First African Americans are not the only Americans that are part of this problem. For example European Americans, Native Americans, and Asian Americans to name just three groups are part of the problem. The "race" problem is not a Black problem it is an American problem, and therefore all Americans of good will need to play a role in solving it.

Once we get by these problematic Subjective Impressions. A third millenium look at America's "race" problem indicates three clear problems. Two of the problems you know, more or less. The third problem is new. So lets move on to our objective and analysis parts of the SOAP Model.

Objectively the CLP diagnoses two major components of the race problem in America, American disharmony, and African American disunity.

Disharmony in America is common knowledge. There are current conflicts between Latino's i.e. Mexican Americans in the southwest to Puerto Ricans in the northeast. Historic conflicts between European Americans and Native Americans and African Americans throughout the country. America has far less harmony than it needs to be an effective Team player in this new global village. The standards and rules enabling a nation to be a competitive moral, economic or military player in the new shrunken world environment have changed. The changes should give America a new incentive for fixing her internal Harmony issues.

Disunity in the African American community keeps a major player on America's team from contributing their full potential to the team's effort. Our research indicates that European Americans believe that African Americans don't have their act together (don't act effectively as a group). Asian Americans echo the same sentiment. That is compared to other groups e.g. Jewish Americans, Italian Americans etc. African Americans are disunited. In fact the harshest critics of the African American group are African Americans themselves. Not one group felt that African Americans were sufficiently unified.

Analysis of the problem reveals **a common cause**. This is where the cultural literacy project analysis differs from the analysis of the "race" problem that is commonly talked and written about in America. The project asserts that disharmony in America and disunity in the African American community have the same cause. We describe this cause as **cultural poisoning** (CP). When we say we have a new idea for America the notion and understanding of cultural poisoning is the heart of this new idea. I mentioned earlier that neither education nor politics, is the fundamental cause of the race problem in America. Our discussion will point out that underneath education, politics and any other elements of the American "race" problem you will find cultural poisoning.

The plan takes it's energy from the point of view that the problem can be fixed. The action plan stage requires providing an antidote to cultural poisoning. Our prognosis is that in curing the pervasive cultural poisoning in Americans, we will best position our countrymen to resolve once and for all the American "race" problem.

So the American "race" problem model has pointed out that cultural poisoning is the underlying cause of America's race problem. The question now becomes **what is cultural poisoning?** We will utilize the second model to help explain the mechanics of cultural poisoning. We call this model the Cultural Literacy Strategy model.

*   *   *

II. THE STRATEGY MODEL

The model is in **two parts.** The first part is a simplified version of the

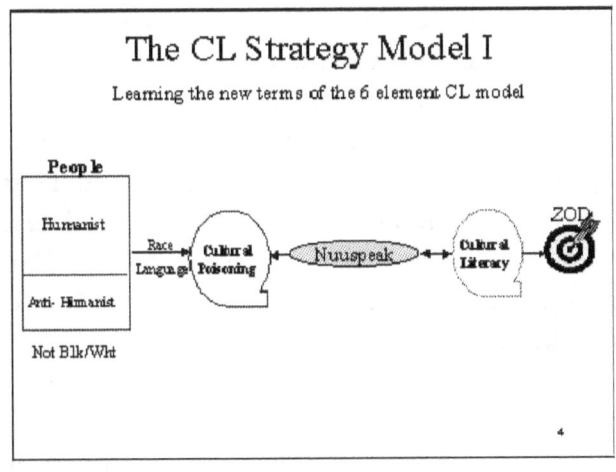

Figure 1 Strategy Model

model designed to get you familiar with some new terms. Once we introduce you to the terms we will use the second part of the model to provide you with more detail on each element and how the elements fit together. One of the things we learned from the project is that there literally are very few words for describing the "race" problem. So we out of necessity have added and/or modified words to describe elements of the race problem, where we found no words existed. In fact, the main obstacle in resolving the race problem, is that there has been no language to assist those working on the problem to connect the dots. The CP Model will help you connect the dots.

The CL Strategy Model has **six elements**. The **first** element is people. You will note that rather than taking the traditional approach of labeling the people as black and white, we describe them as **humanists and anti-humanists**. A humanist is a person who is in favor of life, liberty, and the pursuit of happiness for all. An anti-humanist is a person who is in favor of life, liberty, and the pursuit of happiness for some. The **Second** element, is race language. There is in fact a specialized language we use to talk about "race". However, we do not think of it as such because the words are part of common every day speech. They are words you are already familiar with like Negro, African American, Affirmative Action etc. The **third element,** cultural poisoning is a state of possessing and operating on corrupted cultural information, regarding a particular ethnic group especially one's own. The **fourth element,** Nuuspeak is a new language we will explain in a minute. The **Fifth element,** cultural literacy[vi] is the opposite of cultural poisoning, a state of having accurate information about an ethnic group's culture. Finally we come to the **sixth** and last element, the Zone of Optimal Development (ZOD). Seeing all Americans operating in the ZOD is the ultimate goal of the project. So the CP model starts with people operating at a given level of effectiveness, and ends with them operating at a higher level of effectiveness living in the ZOD. For Team America to realize it's full potential the majority of its players must operate in the ZOD.

Having introduced you to the new terms associated with part one of the CL strategy model we can now move on to **part two.** Part two of the model is the complete model, and will provide you with **more detail about the models** operation. Specifically the complete model describes the psychosocial diagnosis and prescription necessary to correct and move beyond cultural poisoning.

We noted earlier that Cultural Poisoning (CP) is at the bottom of American dis-harmony and African American disunity. We describe **CP as a psychosocial disorder,** that is both an individual psychological disorder and a more general American social disorder. The CL Strategy Model will describe what causes CP (diagnosis) and describe a plan of action to eliminate the disorder (prescription) in which all Americans can participate.

1. People, the first_element in the CP model are infected by the Cultural Aids virus. Physical AIDS means Acquired Immune Deficiency Syndrome. **Cultural** (Psychological) **AIDS** means **Acquired Information Deficiency Syndrome.** By information deficiency we mean that people suffer from a lack of reality, based cultural information about specific cultural groups either in a general sense or a specific sense.

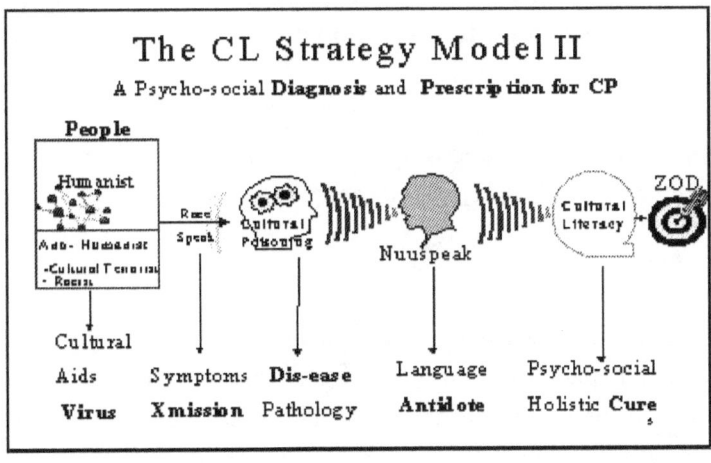

You will recall that the physical pathology of AIDS progresses as follows. An individual is infected by the AIDS virus, which disables his/her biological immune system. A life threatening disease is able to then sneak by the immune system and cause illness or death.

The psychological pathology of AIDS progresses in a similar manner. An individual is infected by the Cultural AIDS virus, which disables his/her psychological immune system. A Cultural-life threatening disease is able to then sneak by the immune system and cause cultural illness or cultural death (and in some cases, physical death).

Obviously anti-humanists are infected with the virus. However, less obvious and more importantly, **humanists are also infected** with the virus. Humanists are the largest human group and are found in every ethnic group. The strategy is focused on what can be done for humanists, verses what can be done against anti-humanists. As we kill off the virus in the humanist group, they will kill off the virus in the smaller Anti-humanist group.

In our model, **racists and cultural terrorists** are simply sub-groups of the anti-humanist group. Racists (believers in the local/global system of White supremacy) display obvious anti-humanistic behavior patterns e.g. card carrying KKK members. Less obvious but more dangerous are the cultural terrorists. They lead those little pointy-headed, white sheet people. They are usually cloaked in the educational professions such as teachers or scholars.

Now that we have explained the components of the first element of the model we will move on to the **second element**.

*   *   *

2. **Race language** previously explained, is called by **the new word race-speak**. RaceSpeak is a specialized language for discussing race in the same sense that computers or medicine have a specialized, dedicated language which makes it easier (more efficient) to discuss those subjects. Computer language promotes efficient thinking, and speech for individuals engaged

in the business or use of computers. As such, it has a positive and expansive effect on computer thought. RaceSpeak in contrast promotes inefficient thinking, and speech regarding issues of "race". As it is currently used racespeak has a negative and **thought contracting effect** on cultural thought.

RaceSpeak is both a symptom and the means of transmitting the cultural AIDS virus. An example of a racespeak symptom is the use of the word Indian to describe Native Americans. The notion of an American Indian has no basis in reality. There are Indians in India but not in America. There are no such people as American Indians. It is a psychological phrase invented to confuse reality. For instance, if you look at a cowboy and "Indian" movie and you believe you are watching good cowboys defeating bad "Indians" you are exhibiting a symptom of a specific form of AIDS, we call Historic AIDS. The reality is you are typically watching European Americans attacking (usually unprovoked) and slaughtering Native Americans. The person using the word "Indian' in the unrealistic context is exhibiting a cultural AIDS symptom. Indian in this case is also the means of transmitting unrealistic cultural information about Native Americans (Cultural AIDS).

The **third element** and the heart of our model is Cultural Poisoning.

3. Cultural Poisoning is the state of maintaining and operating under corrupted cultural information, regarding an ethnic group and their worldviews.[vii] There are two types of cultural poisoning, personal and group poisoning. **Personal poisoning** is the condition wherein a person of a given ethnic group is disconnected from his/her culture. **Group poisoning** is a condition wherein a person and/or a group maintains or operates on culturally corrupt (non-reality based) information about another ethnic group, or their own group. The Star Model of the Three major ethnic groups and their worldview databases is illustrated below.

More will be said about these groups in the body of the book, especially the section dealing with melanin.

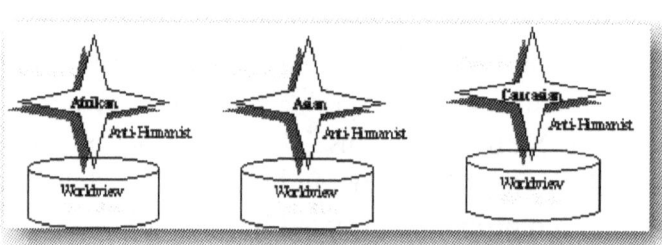

An example of Personal Poisoning is an African American who has been disconnected from their culture, and has had it replaced mostly or entirely by Western culture.

An **example of Group Poisoning** is a European American who has no reality-based information about African American culture, or Asian American culture. Or is misinformed about the full realities of his own culture.

We mentioned earlier that Cultural AIDS disabled **the psychological immune system.** By psychological immune system we mean the psychological programs in one's mind, for example, the true/false program or the good/bad program. If ones capacity to distinguish what is true from what is false is disabled, then some one can easily slip corrupted information in under the wire.

So cultural poisoning is a dis-ease whose pathology is simple. Corrupted language (mis-information, dis-information and omission) causes the dis-ease. **By disease we mean two things,** one is the psychological **disorder** we have been discussing. Second, is the **mental discomfort** from which individuals infected by cultural poisoning suffer. Hatred, prejudice, or other forms of corrupted thinking do not produce a mind at ease but rather a mind that is dis-eased.

I have said that cultural poisoning is at the heart of the "race" problem in America. This is because of the **anti-social behavior** that it is capable of producing. This behavior ranges from mild prejudice to lethal criminally insane behavior (individuals who will kill other human beings because of color or culture).

Anyone, who owns a personal computer and has observed it's irrational behavior, after being infected by a computer virus, has a sense of the dramatic effects cultural poisoning can have on the human bio-computer, and man's behavior toward his fellow man.

Now you have a basic understanding of the third element of the cultural poisoning model. It is a psychosocial disorder and can be lethal. We will talk about this in more detail in the racespeak section of this book. Now lets move onto the **fourth element** of the model, Nuuspeak.

4. Nuuspeak is a new language designed to be an antidote to cultural poisoning, and a vaccine against racespeak. By antidote we mean clear language connected to reality to counteract cultural poisoning. Nuuspeak has a growing number of words and phrases that have been thrown up by people interested in the CLP as well as from the general culturally literate. **Examples:** Humanist and Anti-Humanist vs. the traditional Black and White divisions, Cultural Poisoning and Cultural Literacy, Classical African Civilization, cultural terrorist, biological Blackness vs. psychological Blackness, Afrophobia- irrational fear of Blacks, etc. So on one level nuuspeak, as an antidote is a language correction to counter the effects of dis-information, omission and misinformation that are presently part of racespeak.

Nuuspeak as a vaccine is a form of protection against the ill effects of racespeak. That is to the extent you are fortified with ethnic, reality based information, you are vaccinated against the corrupted **information of racespeak. Cultural poisoning is a** malignant disease that is commonly passed on to children by their infected parents. If you cure yourself, one of the first things you might want to do is vaccinate your children. Would it not be remarkable if Cultural Poisoning was eradicated and third millenium children grew up without this disability in the new global village?

Now that we have dealt with the antidote and vaccine qualities of the fourth element of the model, we will move to the **fifth element,** Cultural Literacy.

5. Cultural Literacy is understanding your culture and being able to distinguish it's accumulated values, interests, and principles (VIP) from that of other cultures. This implies that not only must you understand your own culture, but also you must have at least a functional knowledge of at least one other culture. For example African Americans should understand their culture from Classical African Civilization to the present along with its traditional VIP's. They should also be able to distinguish their culture and VIP's from European American culture (Greek classical culture to the present) or from Asian American culture (Asian classical civilization to present). Knowing your culture, and having a functional understanding of the culture of others breeds mutual respect. This type of respect is quite different than the current "color blind" political correctness that promotes neither understanding, nor respect of other cultures.

Cultural literacy is cultural health. CL is the traditional glue that holds a people together around shared Values, Interests, and Principles (VIP's). When a people have shared VIP's you don't have to advocate for better unity for it is automatic. For instance no one need advocate for Jewish unity. Their traditional shared VIP's makes their unity automatic on the important group issues.

So cultural literacy is understanding your culture, and that of others with whom you live and work. CL is **indispensable to producing unity** within an ethnic group and mutual respect and harmony in a multiethnic society. One of the things we have learned in the cultural literacy project is that you can not effectively implement **cultural literacy in the bio-computer of a culturally poisoned individual.** There are simply too many bad programs running. You must eradicate CP before you can inject cultural literacy into an individual.

In this model cultural literacy is the cure. We call it **a psychosocial holistic cure**. Psycho, because it improves the psychological health of the individual. Social because it improves the intra and inter ethnic behavior of individuals and groups. We refer to it as a holistic cure, because it is not a point solution like education or political effectiveness. Getting everyone "educated" is a partial solution. Education in America has degenerated into simply training for a job. It provides relatively little reality-based information on how to be a good human being and how to get along with ones fellow countrymen. The truth of this statement lies in the fact that, disharmony in America persists despite the remarkable rise in the "educational" level of Americans since the country's inception.

Cultural literacy on the other hand by default will **produce more educationally and politically effective American citizens**. People who are more knowledgeable about their culture and that of others, by default are better educated. They also tend to make better use of educational and political opportunities.

At this point we have learned that the cultural literacy strategy proposed the fifth element of the model as the cure to America's "race" problem. We have also noted that CL can not be effectively implemented while cultural poisoning contaminates the psychological and social environment in America.

We can now move on to the **<u>sixth and final element</u>** of the Cultural Literacy Strategy Model. It is the goal of the CL Strategy we call the ZOD.

6. The Zone of Optimal Development (ZOD) is a psychological /spiritual state of mind, where based on knowledge one is able to maximize one's human potential. In the classical African civilization it was called "becoming Ausar". Ausar the fully developed human being.

ZOD strategy is a combination of African and American development processes. These culturally neutral processes are a summary of successful personal development models. They can assist individuals and their groups maximize their political, economic, and social effectiveness. This is the ultimate goal of the CLP for all Americans.

To summarize the CL Strategy Model. The model has six elements starting with (1) people infected by the cultural AIDS virus. (2) Racespeak i.e. the way we talk about "race" and race issues today. (3) Cultural Poisoning, the absence of reality based cultural information. (4) Nuuspeak, the antidote to CP. (5) Cultural Literacy, the cure for America's "race" problem and (6) the goal is to follow the yellow brick road to the ZOD.

*   *   *

Now that you are familiar with the American "race" problem Model and the CL Strategy designed to combat the problem, lets look at **how implementing the strategy will impact America's "race" problem.**

The American "race" problem Model depicts the fact that there are two Objective problems, which inhibit American progress. Those are disharmony, and disunity. It points out that the problems have the same root, Cultural Poisoning. To address the problems indicated, the Project proposes the **CL Strategy as a plan of action** to be used to eradicate America's "race" problem.

The strategy describes CP and the **antidote to CP**. While the antidote can reduce, or eliminate CP, it does not in and of it self restore an individual to cultural health. To return to health, one needs an **injection of cultural literacy**. This "race" problem model shows the projected effects of the CL Strategy, creating the ideal, harmonious American environment in the form of an Aunk (Afrikan Key to life). **The Aunk result** depicts the assertion, that if America takes the medicine prescribed by the CL Strategy, it will result in natural African American unity held together by the glue of cultural literacy. Unified African Americans will be more effective Team America players capable of leading the drive for harmony, in the larger American community. **Unity and harmony will move America** down the yellow brick road **to the ZOD** and closer to her goal of becoming a morally, politically, and economically effective citizen of the global village.

Said another way, African **Americans must get their own act together** if they expect to effectively impact harmony in the larger community. The "race" problem in America is not an African American problem that only African Americans must fix. No doubt African Americans have their own ethnic specific work to do. However, **the problem is an American problem**, which all humanists must participate in fixing, if America is to finally and fully resolve her ethnic conflicts.

*   *   *

In summary we will end as we began, by answering the three questions we started out to answer regarding the final solution to America "race" problem.

What's the Problem?—**Cultural Poisoning**

What's the fix?—**Nuuspeak and Cultural Literacy**

What's in it for you?—**True Peace** which is the (Key to Life)

Leading us all; you, family, group and nation to the goal of living in the **ZOD**

The question is what time is it? You are here "**X**", and we have a new idea, so lets get busy!

Ok, **Now that you have completed the Cultural Literacy Project Overview.** You have a working knowledge of the goals, objectives, strategies and tactics of the project. The project proposed, for your consideration, a fresh analysis and diagnosis of the problem and a new prescription and a hopeful prognosis for the future.

So up to this point in the book you have taken the test, read the preface, and CLP Overview. I hope this has given you a good feel for the new realities of "Race" in the third millenium. New realities require new tools and new solutions. I hope that our youth (Hip-Hop Generation) in particular will pick up these tools and help us provide America with new solutions in the context of their realities.

To assist in this process I intend to provide you with three books I affectionately describe as the Cultural Literacy Trilogy. DoubleSpeak is the first of these books. The Last page of the Overview will introduce you to the Trilogy. It will show you how each book fits into the Cultural Literacy Strategy Model. That is what part of the CL Strategy each book is intended to cover. Hopefully this will give you a context for where we both are in this new millenium discussion at this point in time. You will also find on the next page how to reach me and other cultural soldiers in cyberspace.

*   *   *

The **cultural literacy trilogy** is a series of books designed to convey the good, the bad, and the ugly of our proposed personal action based solution. The first two books, are informational and start you on your cultural literacy journey starting with the cultural poisoning self-test. The second book, restores your right to know about the origins of your culture. The third book 2084 is a novel with a vision of the future.

The Cultural Literacy Trilogy
From the honorable Ancestors directly to you

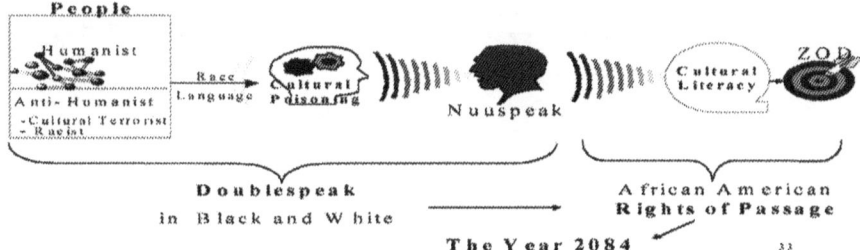

Doublespeak BW: explains Cultural Poisoning and the antidote

AA Rites of Passage: provides a road map to Cultural Literacy
Understanding Classical African Civilization (CAC)

2084: Demonstrates two visions of the future:
How the world will look if we take the medicine
How the world will look if we fail to take the medicine

Actions speak louder than words, WHAT ARE YOU GOING TO DO?
The first step is taking the cultural poisoning self-test.
Contact us at E-Mail raunk@iname.com Web Site Cultural Literacy
Central http://come.to/aunk

Introduction to the Cultural Poisoning Self Test

As we discussed in the Cultural Literacy Project Overview the CL Self-Test is **the first step** an individual should take to activate the cultural literacy strategy. The road to resolving the "race" problem in America starts with each American taking a hard look at themselves, and the beliefs they hold. The road to Team America is not an easy one, otherwise we would have already arrived at our destination. Some of what you read may offend you, that is not my intent. You must keep in mind as you read that this journey will require for many, considerable tolerance for the beliefs of others and an open mind to new ideas.

Before you start to review the answers allow me to **thank you** for taking the self-test. You have just taken a new step down the path to Cultural Literacy. Now let me tell you a little **about the purpose and structure of the self-test**. First, if you have not written down your answers please do so <u>now</u>! This will provide you with a written record of your original ideas for reference.

It really is important that you think about each question, reach a conclusion, or realize that you have no opinion on a given topic. Write down your answer so you have a permanent one or two word (number) answer that represents your thinking on the issue.

The **purpose** of the self-test is to **have you demonstrate to yourself that the information you and I have learned over the years is not necessarily the truth** (in agreement with reality). Cultural Literacy is not something someone can give you—it is something you give yourself. It is a process of changing your way of thinking. **The purpose of this self-test and the book is to help you jumpstart that thinking process.**

The **structure** of the self-test is simple. **You provide some ideas, I provide some ideas, and together we think about them.** Whenever you are asked a question you can only arrive at one of three conclusions. Either you know the answer, you do not know the answer, or you are not sure whether or not you know the answer. The fact that you can only logically reach one of three conclusions regarding a question may seem rudimentary to many readers however, there are far too many people who do not have this basic **three-conclusion rule** in their thinking tool bag. Our research indicates that many Americans literally delude themselves about what they know and don't know.

Our youth call this delusion **"fronting"**. Someone who is fronting is trying to get others to believe something that is not true. For example, they may try to get others to believe that they have a lot of money when they don't. Or that they are players when they know they are not. In the case of **self-delusion,** the individual who is fronting may not be clear in their own mind about the truth, or falsehood, of what they believe or are saying to others.

For you to get maximum benefit out of the information presented you must continuously apply the three-conclusion rule. If you did not apply the rules to the questions go back and do it now. As you read the answers, come to a firm conclusion on each new piece of information you receive. That is you find the information to be true (agrees with reality, the facts support it) or false (the facts don't support it or you suspend judgement (you don't have enough facts and you are unsure). So I am asking you to be as clear as you can be about your conclusions. The three-conclusion rule requires that when you receive new information you conclude that it is true, false, or you suspend judgement pending the receipt of more facts.

The three-conclusion rule is indispensable to critical thinking and will serve you well in all things you are required to think about from your job to your religion.

The set of ideas (information) I am providing as **my input** is not entirely my own. They are rather a compilation of ideas **from** the settled body of knowledge already established in what is termed **the African Centered Movement** (Afrocentric). My input will typically be **in two parts**: Ideas (information) regarding the **specific question,** and **more general information** regarding a **bigger question,** that the specific question raises. The Bigger question is intended to alert you and start you thinking about the underlying reasons for some of the beliefs we hold. The bigger questions are dealt with, in limited fashion in this book due to space limitations.

Although I am not with you as you read our book, I hope that the part of **my spirit** that is responsible for thinking, and that part of **your spirit** that is responsible for thinking, will **join together** and have a fruitful conversation.

*   *   *

Having introduced you to the **purpose and structure** of the self-test, **let's begin the discussion** regarding our beliefs and opinions.

Just because we have been taught, or come to believe something, does not make it so, even if all the people you know believe it to be so. The flat earth people all believed the earth was flat. The truth is that the earth is round. The earth was round before the flat earth people thought it was flat and after they figured out the truth of its roundness.

The point of the flat earth analogy is that the truth is not relative. The truth is what it is. You are in possession of the truth when what is in your mind agrees with reality. However, we may have ideas in our heads that fall short of the truth. That is, we may hold beliefs that we are attached to or opinions that we have arrived at, or simply tastes that we prefer. For example, I like brown rice for no other reason then that I like brown rice. Taste is the weakest form of truth, and requires no reason or proof. Beliefs and opinions require a reason for you holding them. **The question is, are the ideas you hold consistent with the truth?** If they are not, then why not, and what are you going to do about it?

Applying the three-conclusion rule is part of the answer to what you should be doing about it.

The purpose of the self-test is to cause you to **think** about the reasons that you hold certain beliefs, or opinions. I am asking you to do five things, should you decide to accept the challenge:

1. **Look** at the ideas you presently hold by answering the ten questions.
2. **Think** about the ideas presented to you in the answers.
3. **Compare** your beliefs and opinions to the answers.
4. **Consider** whether or not you need to adjust your beliefs and/or opinions regarding the ten subjects.
5. **Decide** what the self-test experience means to you, your ethnic group, and Team America.

After the self-test the book will present you with three "ALERTS". The alerts are not really chapters or sections. The information in these three area's of the book are intended to alert you to the existence of information you need to know more about.

The first alert is on racespeak. It presents you with a graphic we call the Racespeak Model. The model alerts you to the fact that there is a standard way of determining if any word, or phrase is a positive or negative racespeak word.

The Second alert is on the cultural war. It presents you with a table, that transforms the little understood widely used term "cultural war" into a structural model that is easier to think about and work with.

The third alert is on the Aunk. It alerts you to the fact that the Aunk is not just a popular ancient symbol but a universal model that can be applied to many things.

At this point you have been introduced to the, Cultural Literacy Project which provides the context for the information we will be discussing. You also have an introduction to the information we will be discussing in this book. So now it is time to get to the heart of the matter, the individual questions and answers.

Gook luck! Hopefully you will find the information presented very valuable as you travel the road to Cultural Literacy.

The Self Test Questions and Answers

1. Maps

Were all the maps we learned from in school more or less accurate? NO

The Flat Map Myth goes something like this. You will all remember your teachers telling you something like "…the map we are using is not accurate…the distortions happen when you take a round globe and flatten it out. This process makes the world slightly distorted". This was not a myth. It was and is a down right LIE. By lie I mean the truth of how landmasses are arranged on the planet has been corrupted, misrepresented, by the popular flat map that most of us learned from in school, and those distortions were created very purposefully.

The people responsible for teaching us about the world told us two things and left out one. (1) **The map is distorted**—TRUE. (2) The REASON for the **distortion is because the round world was made flat**—misinformation (not the whole truth). (3) The third part of the map lie is **omission**. The "teacher" failed to mention exactly what it is about the map that is distorted. Not only that, the non-scientific reasons for the particular distortions were also left out.

The Truth is Cartography is not a haphazard process. It is a high—tech, precise science. A cartographer does not sit around making roughly accurate maps, or trying to unroll the paper from a round globe in order to turn it into a flat map. **Pilots do not fly,**

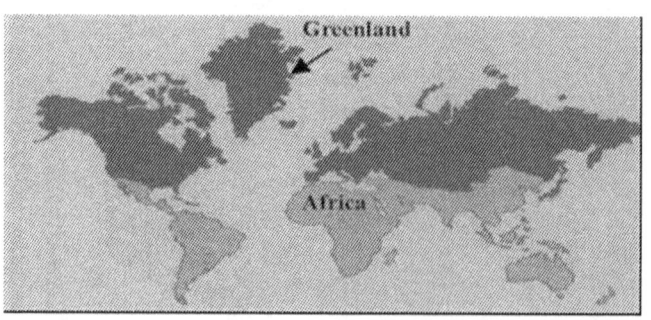

and ship captains do not sail based on distorted maps. So why is it that our children are learning from distorted maps? The answer is Cultural Poisoning.

The map we learned in school is called the Mercator map (figure 12). It is **not accurate**. It is drawn so that the northern portion of the map appears to be 2/3 of the earth's surface, and the southern portion 1/3. This is the **opposite of reality**. It is in fact a subtle form of geographic reverse psychology. No pilot would be able to use this map to find his/her way around the world because of the fact that it is so distorted. Like most people, I grew up using this map and **never thought to question** the accuracy of this representation of the earth.

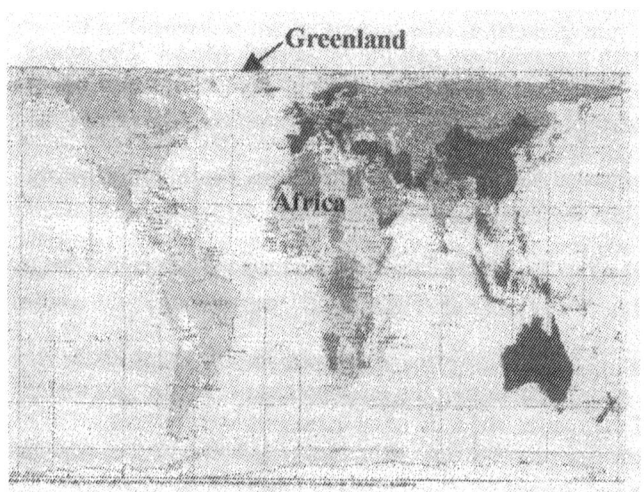

Not one teacher in high school, or college **ever told me I could not find my way to the bathroom with this map.**

What was the **result for me?** For most of my life, I took for granted that the land inhabited by White people was larger and more populated than the land inhabited by people of color. It made sense to me then, that most of the people in the world were White since most of the people on T.V. were also White. The **truth is that people of color far outnumber White people in the world**. So from a worldview perspective, White people are actually the minorities. Isn't it interesting how one piece of dis-information (a distorted map), can effect other pieces of information your mind holds regarding reality?

There is an accurate map. It is called the Peters map (figure 13). The landmasses are drawn as an accurate reflection of the proportions found in reality. The United Nations has begun using the accurate map. I had occasion to call my son's high school to encourage them to also use the Peters map, so that my son would not suffer the same cultural poisoning I suffered. Rather than the argument, I expected, I found that the school too had recently adapted the Peters map.

The Peters Map has four elements, which correct the distortions of the Mercator map.

Equal Area: Countries, continents and oceans are shown according to their actual size. This enables accurate comparisons of the three major components of the map.

Equal Axis: North /South lines are vertical, enabling you to tell the precise direction from one point on the map to any other point on the map.

Equal Positions: East /West lines are parallel, enabling the viewer to determine the relationship of any point on the map, such as its distance from the equator or its angle to the sun.

Truth crushed to earth will rise again: By depicting all countries in their true size and location, "distortion" is replaced by truth. No small country is counterfeited to look big, and no big country is countrified to look small. A lie is replaced by the truth, which is always a great day for mankind.

Who chose the map and what was the purpose of having everyone use an inaccurate map when an accurate one was/is available and known to scholars? More importantly, why is the Mercator map still more widely used than the Peters all over the world? To plant and perpetuate the myth of White supremacy. The fake map is a part of Cultural Poisoning. It is pictographic image poisoning with a purpose. Negative Racespeak is not restricted to words; racespeak can also be images.

By the way, in case you didn't know; the small island of Greenland (0.8 mil. Sq. mil.), is not almost as large as Africa (11.6 Mill. Sq. Miles) as the

Mercator Map inaccurately portrays. The Mercator map was put into play during a time when Europe dominated and exploited the world. See figure 12 & 13 the little island of Greenland is labeled; look at the drastic difference in size for the same unchanging physical place on the planet.

The flat map myth teaches us something about how truth, and falsehood work as a general proposition. There are **three main modes of corrupting the truth. They are** misinformation, dis-information, and omission. If the teacher did not know of the existence of a more accurate map, then she simply **misinformed you**; no malice intended. In that case the teacher also having been duped was parroting or passing on corrupted information. On the other hand, the professional map maker who's job it is to know about all the different types of maps **dis-informs you,** when they purposely send the inaccurate map into schools. This person is not accidentally misinforming you. The professional knows the difference between truth, and falsehood and chooses not to tell you the truth (dis-inform)

The third form of corrupting the truth is **omission.** That means to leave out important information. So when the teacher tells you the map is distorted but omits the part of why this is so, then he or she has prevented you from knowing the whole truth by leaving part of it out.

The second mode of corrupting information, **dis-information has two variations** that are important to distinguish. In the first instance the dis-informer can **modify reality**. In the second instance the dis-informer can actually **create reality**. How does this work, a quote from the wall version of the peters map is instructive.

"While the peters map is superior in its portrayal of proportions and sizes, it's importance goes far beyond its cartographic accuracy. Nothing less then our world view is at stake".

The great cultural poisoning danger of the Mercator map is not its physical inaccuracy. Its real danger is its **capacity to distort worldview realities**. The Mercator map can be seen hanging in corporate boardrooms, and behind the anchorman on your local or major news stations. This continuous misrepresentation of the world geography produces views about cultures, and the places on the planet from whence they originate and/or are concentrated which are completely disconnected from reality. It is this subtle form of cultural poisoning not just the more obvious stereotyping that poses the greatest threat to one's connection to truth and reality.

Have you figured out how the **flat map myth relates to the cultural poisoning model**? The flat map myth is part of a specific strain of cultural AIDS called geographic AIDS which, can mutate into worldview AIDS (WVA). WVA is a distorted view of the world. These forms of the virus disrupt the reality programs running in an individual's bio-computer. They can cause the individual to reach erroneous conclusions based on his misperceptions. In our discussion, I used my youthful conclusions about the world, as an example of how **misperception can lead to faulty judgments** in ones worldview.

How do we neutralize the viruses and eradicate the cultural poisoning? We take the antidote, which is always, truth (reality). In this specific case we replace the inaccurate Mercator map with the more accurate Peters map.

The area of the earth above the equator is not 2/3 bigger then the area below the equator. Don't let anybody including your parents tell you differently. **Reality is reality: THINK FOR YOUR SELF!**

$$* \qquad\qquad * \qquad\qquad *$$

The Bigger Question: The Big is Small Trick
Something to think about

If cultural poisoning can trick you on something so basic as the way land is arranged on the planet, then what else have you been tricked about? **What other information have you been duped with?**

Malcolm X speaking to African Americans often said you have been duped, hood winked! And although the term cultural poisoning had yet to be invented, he was right in describing the effects of just that. The American "race" problem model which looks beyond just the African American group makes the point, that not just African Americans have been duped, but so have Asian Americans as well as European Americans. In Fact, **the Mercator map dupes all Americans.** Everyone's view of the world and their capacity to make clear cultural assessments and judgements is damaged by inaccurate information.

So how do we **cure cultural poisoning? One virus at a time**. Each one teaches one. You now have a more accurate flat map representation of the world, so you have the antidote to this particular virus in your hands. **Give the antidote to your children** so that they are vaccinated against this particular strain of the virus. Something else may distort their view of the world, but it should no longer be the Mercator map.

The Peters literature points out that the U.N., local schools, and at least one American State has adapted the more accurate map as their official map. What about your local school or state? **America <u>can</u> identify and neutralize cultural viruses.** If we neutralize enough of them we can cure cultural poisoning in America.

Note: Remember, as I mentioned in the preface, **Doublespeak In Black And White's limited space and scope** allows only a brief mentioning of the "bigger questions". So as a kind of cultural-alert, at the end of each question, I will cover at least one of the bigger questions raised by the basic questions. This is intended to serve as food for thought until I have an opportunity to talk to you more fully about the subject.

2. Number of Continents

How many continents are there in the world? 6. Is Europe one on them? NO

The most common answer to the first part of this question is 7. WHY? The most common answer to the second part of the question is **YES**

A continent, according to the dictionary, is **one of the earth's major divisions of land** surrounded mostly by water. A quick glance at any world map including the infamous Mercator map, will show that there are **only six major bodies of land that fit that description.** They are (1) Asia, (2) Africa, (3) North America, (4) South America (5) Australia, and (6) Antarctica.

So what is the myth-logical continent that we have been duped into belie-ving exi-sts? It is Europe. If

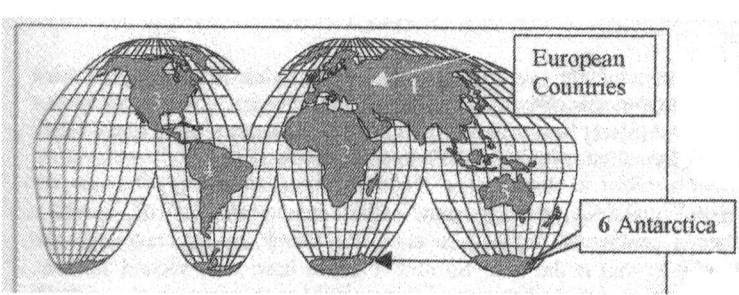

Figure 4 Map of the major bodies of land in the world

you ans-wered that Europe is one of the continents, you answered with the majority of those who took this test during our research. You don't need to be an expert in geography to know Europe does not meet the definition. You only need to use your eyes. **Europe is not a continent.**

Around 175 million years ago, there was one huge super continent called Pangaea[viii]. It was completely surrounded by water. Pangaea broke up into the six geographic continents that have made up the earth for millions of years. So where is the seventh (7) continent? **India is sometimes called the sub-continent,** because in the history of land movement on planet earth it was at one time a major body of land completely surrounded by water. It eventually attached itself to Asia and is now part of southern Asia. The area of Asia called **Europe has no such geographical history** and can not even be qualified as a sub-continent, let alone a continent. The words "European Continent" are a form of doublespeak, which misrepresent reality.

Unless there is **a major geological event** in which a lot of land breaks off from one of the six continents, then there is and never will be a seventh continent.

Isn't it interesting that white people can tell the world anything, and we assume it is true without any regard for what is evidenced by reality? It is a normal propensity of the human mind to check information it receives with reality. So why have so many people's bio-computer failed to check when someone fed them the seven continent myth? The answer is cultural poisoning.

Europe is a relatively small area of land attached to the western end of Asia. In my research, on occasion, I would hear people refer to the continent of **Eurasia.** While this appears to be less blatantly insulting to one's intelligence it is still a falsehood (modified doublespeak), because **there is no such continent** . **The name of the continent is Asia.** There is an area of Western Asia, which consists of "European" countries like England, France, and Italy. That can be properly called Europe. You will certainly notice that the word "Eurasia" denotes the fact that the European countries are on the continent of Asia. It is interesting to note that the same people who mandate that our children be taught the false reality of seven continents (including the European continent), are the same people who created the word Eurasia.

This notion of **Europe being a continent came about in a time** when Europeans were leaving the area of Western Asia to attack, enslave and subjugate other people. It is understandable that White supremacists, who embarked on a worldwide campaign of slash and burn, would want to increase their cultural standing in the world by inventing a continent for themselves. While we can understand it, that does not mean we should buy it!

This type of dis-information results in another type of AIDS virus called Geographic AIDS.

One of the remarkable things about becoming culturally literate is that you run across the most interesting psychological devices. When you come to something, which does not seem to agree with your perception of reality, you **look to make the argument for or against that new information.** In the case of the European continental myth it is not that the argument is weak, illogical, or poorly thought out for there simply is no argument. Just as their would be no rational argument, we could mount as Americans if we decided to all of a sudden call the New England states a continent, just because they sort of stuck out into the water. Most rational people in the world would not buy or appreciate us designating New England as the new 7th or 8th continent. At least I hope they would not. Most thinking people would recognize that for exactly what it would be, a **non-reality created out of thin air.** And any notion of Europe as a continent is just that.

In the previous question on maps, we learned that the average individual is susceptible to cultural poisoning, and that dis-information is one of the three modes of lying. We learned that the Mercator Map tricked us with a variation of dis-information by **"falsely modifying reality"**. The European continental myth represents the second variation of dis-information, which is called **"creating reality"**.

The antidote to the "created reality" mutation of Geographic AIDS, once again, is truth (reality). Specifically the antidote to the "seven continents" myth is to know that there are six continents and knowing the scientific reality behind why that is the case. So now that you have your second antidote, vaccinate your self and your children. If you don't have any children vaccinate someone else's child. Remember the old African proverb, It takes a village to raise a child. By the way this ancient proverb has some interesting implications as we start to think about the new global village, which requires that we "really" know where things and people are on the planet

*   *   *

The Bigger Question: Reality Control 2 + 2 = 5

Freedom is the ability to say **2+2 = 4** even when someone is telling you that it is **five**. **Reality Control is a critical concept** necessary to understanding cultural poisoning. Many Blacks are convinced that there is a **conspiracy** of some number of White men that talk to each other and adversely effect Blacks. I assert that the apparent conspiratorial behavior exhibited by some Whites is not perpetrated by a group of **White men in a room**. Rather it is a universal way of thinking known as a **worldview**. People who share the same worldview—western, eastern or southern—tend to think and behave in a similar way regarding certain subjects. For example note the different reactions from Blacks and Whites regarding the O.J. Simpson "Trial of the Century".

It is interesting to note that if you **look up "continent" in the dictionary** it is not uncommon to find the **counterfeit continent** Europe used as an example of the word. Now did the mapmakers conspire with the dictionary makers? Probably not, however they shared the same worldview and therefore perpetrated the same misinformation.

It is important to understand that it is not necessary for two anti-humanists to talk to each other in order **to constitute a conspiracy.** All they have to do is have the same worldview for both of them to think and behave in a unified fashion towards the same end. It is their shared worldview that dictates their thinking as well as their behavioral tendencies.

In our discussion on the mythological European continent, it was my intention to point out to those American youth who may be in high school or college, a specific example of cultural AIDS that would be fresh in their minds. For those out of school, at least you **now know where you caught the reality poisoning** in the first place.

We were told in school that Europe is a continent, and that when asked the question on a test, "how many continents are there?" one should answer seven. I know of at least one teacher who knew that this was not the truth, yet taught it anyway. So we have teachers who are not doing their job, or don't know their job, students who just go along with the program, and parents who have absolutely no idea what their children are learning in school. Unfortunately when I went to school, too often I did the same thing; I took in information without checking its source or validity. I call this parrot AIDS. It is both a teaching and learning disorder.

If you suffer from Parrot AIDS, now that you know what it is, cure yourself and vaccinate your children. If you're inclined to minimize the importance of taking the antidote to Parrot AIDS, I would remind you of the notorious anti-humanist and White supremacist **Hitler.** You will recall he created a new reality out of thin air he called the "Aryan race". Hitler and other anti-humanists then went on to culturally poison other Germans suffering from Parrot AIDS, which took them to the acute stage of criminal insanity. In that mind altered, culturally poisoned state they went out and murdered six million other human beings and then stole their property.

∗   ∗   ∗

To summarize what we learned in question two; we need to review **the first question** for a minute. In question one (the Map question) we identified a specific cultural virus strain, Geographic AIDS, and demonstrated how it produces a specific form of cultural poisoning called geographic poisoning (GP). GP is the information deficiency regarding how land is arranged on the planet. We explained that **GP disrupts the true/false program** running in one's bio-computer, or makes it more susceptible to infection by other strains of AIDS. In this case it is Worldview poisoning (**WVP**). That is WVP corrupted our geographical, and cultural perception of the Northern Hemisphere of the planet.

Question one's geographic AIDS "**modifies reality**". Antidote, the Peters Map.
Question two's geographic AIDS "**invents reality**". Antidote, 6 continent reality

In question two, we discussed how geographic AIDS could mutate into the "invented reality" variation. It is this concept of "**mutation**" that **can be extremely dangerous**. We pointed out that basic worldview AIDS can be mutated into more virulent strains like, **White supremacist AIDS and anti-Semitic AIDS**. We used Hitler as an example of how White supremacist AIDS can induce an acute form of cultural poisoning that is capable of modifying human behavior in such a drastic way, as to cause someone to go out and kill other human beings for "cultural reasons". Naturally, these capacities to create man made psychological viruses, and inject them into the conscious and subconscious of other human beings, inducing them to attack another ethnic group is **not limited in its application to the Jewish ethnic group**.

From this question forward there will be a **summary at the end of each question**. These summaries will be called cultural poisoning "Snap shots". Abbreviated CP Snap Shot. These snap shots will remind you of what you have covered at a given point in the test/answers and what is coming next

Now we are going to **move on to question three**, regarding Classical African Civilization. In the first two questions we examined how cultural AIDS can impact one's perception regarding Western culture. In question three, we will examine how geographic aids can impact ones perception of other cultures by demonstrating its impact on African culture.

3. Where is Classical African Civilization?

In what country is Classical African Civilization located? Kamit (Egypt)

The first thing you should notice about the answer is that I used the name that the ancient Afrikans created for their country, **"Kamit"** and I put **"Egypt" the name that the Greeks called Kamit** in parenthesis. This is the opposite of how it is written in most American books. I do this for **two reasons** that are related to developing antidotes to cultural poisoning. **First, as a humanist,** I respect other human beings and their culture, and will tend to use the same names that indigenous people have given their things and land areas. Typically, I have found no logical, rational, or spiritual reason for arbitrarily changing original names. **Second as an African American** I would naturally call things by the same name that my ancestors called them. That is why the Greek word Egypt is parenthetical.

If you answered this question with either Kamit (Hieroglyphic Kmt) or Egypt give yourself **100% credit**. If you answered "Ta-marry" even though that is not the answer I was asking for it is also correct. If you got this one wrong you are in the company of most Americans who do not know the original name of the country, because they do not know that there is such a reality as the Classical African Civilization.

Awareness of Classical Afrikan Civilization once known, loved and respected throughout the civilized world has been systematically removed from the minds of men. Here in America, it is like someone took a bottle of white out and **whited out the name Kamit,** and the great African civilization it represents from "all" dictionaries, history and religious books.

A particularly disheartening part of my research was finding that fewer then 10% of African Americans questioned knew anything at all about their classical civilization. We call this information deficiency in the general sense **cultural aids**. In the ethnic specific sense it is called **African**

cultural AIDS. That is an information deficit regarding African culture. All three major American ethnic groups suffered from African cultural AIDS at or above the 90% level. However, they did not all suffer the more basic form of the virus, cultural AIDS. That is most groups knew something about their own ethnic group's culture.

When European Americans were asked "tell me about your culture?" most would say that their culture starts with Classical European Civilization in the country of **Greece** and comes to America by way of Europe. **Asian's** would respond that their culture comes from their classical civilization the **Shang dynasty** in China, or they would site some other figure from their classical culture like Confucius. While different Asian groups answered differently all were pretty clear about their own culture. Neither group knew much about African American culture beyond tribe's in Africa and their enslavement in America.

African Americans had a broad range of **inconsistent notions about their culture.** Some simply said American. Some started with "slavery" forward. Others pointed to a West African nation or the Caribbean. And traditional Africans who have recently become African Americans could typically describe the culture of the country in Africa they came from. Less than ten percent could point to their Classical African Civilization Kamit, in the same culturally decisive way that say European Americans could point to Greece.

Why do African Americans have little or no information about their classical civilization? One answer is that knowledge of African culture was systematically destroyed during the enslavement process. But that is only part of the truth. For the first time in thousands of years we now have a clear and fully descriptive answer **"Cultural Poisoning".**

Cultural poisoning started long before the 1500's and the attack on Africa culminating in the enslavement of African Americans (prisoners of war) here in America. We will discuss that issue in the section of the book that describes the cultural war. What is important to understand here is that present day African Americans, like the Native Americans have suffered near cultural genocide.

The fact that **African Americans are culturally poisoned** has a specific root, two very virulent man made strains of AIDS, Kamit out of Africa AIDS **(KO AIDS)** and **Mixed Egyptian AIDS.** Since we are in America we are going to focus on what Americans have done, and are doing to aid and abet in these cultural crimes.

Kamit out of Afrika AIDS is **an attempt to take Kamit (Egypt) out of Africa,** by creating a new geographic area called the "Middle East". This new geographic invention includes the land occupied by biologically mixed people known as Arabs. It includes countries like Arabia, Palestine, Iraq, Egypt etc. The term **"Middle East" is** purposely used to replace the word Africa when referring to modern day Egypt or ancient Kamit.

European American "Scholars", college professors, high school "teachers" and news anchorpersons are carriers and transmitters of KO AIDS.

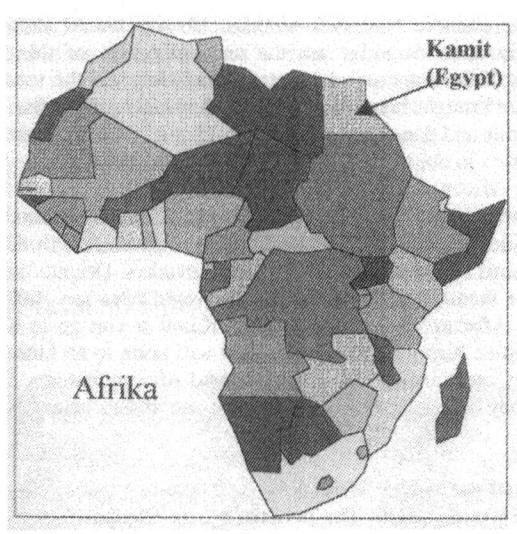

One of the most recent examples is an author by the name of Mary Lefkowitz who wrote the infamous book *Not Out of Africa.* These individuals constantly refer to Egypt as being in the "Middle East". They don't use the African Name Kamit unless forced to do so in some technical context, in which they must write or discuss the subject. This is why modern African Americans do not know the original name of their classical culture, or even that the modern country that contains the great pyramids, known to most as Egypt, is actually in Africa. For those Americans who were not clear about where Kamit (Egypt) is located, let me give you the "antidote" by making it perfectly clear.

Yesterday Kamit (Egypt) was in Africa. If you should happen to check today, Egypt is still in Africa. I have every confidence that Egypt will still be on the continent of Africa tomorrow. It is not—I repeat—**it is not in the "Middle East"**. The Middle East is an **artificial construct of westerners**. It bears no resemblance to the reality of geography. (East of what? Middle of what?) Is Egypt supposed to be east of Africa?

The part of the world often referred to as the "Middle East" is part of the continent of Asia. **South Central Asia** to be exact. Just as Texas is part of the South Central United States. And Kamit (Egypt) is actually in Northeastern Afrika.

This is one of the most blatant clever and successful executions of cultural poisoning in the history of the world. Every African historian or Egyptologists who has addressed this question says the same thing[ix], "the designation "Middle East" has been used to **attempt to take Kamit (Egypt) out of Africa**". All Americans should learn to recognize the phrase "Middle East" as doublespeak.

This is what we mean by Kamit out of Africa AIDS. All Americans through their education and T.V. have been subjected to continuous doses of dis-information, misinformation, and omission regarding Kamit (Egypt). The fact that **KO AIDS is spread by anti-humanists** is obvious. Less obvious but more important is that American scholars, and teachers who would categorize themselves as **humanists are the largest group** of individuals carrying and spreading anti-Kametic virus strains.

The Antidote to KO Aids is being able to see the cultural knock out punch coming. The use of "Middle East" to avoid saying that Kamit (Egypt) is in Africa is an attempt to knock Classical African Civilization out of Africa and out of the world of competitive ideas. KO Aids is also an attempt to knock the reality of a Classical African Civilization out of the minds of men. If the words of negative racespeak have been successful in knocking the idea out of your mind take the antidote and inoculate you children.

This brings us to **the second virus** that block African Americans, and others from learning about Classical African Civilization and culture. Mixed Egyptian AIDS.

Mixed Egyptian AIDS is part of a propaganda campaign to confuse Americans, and the people of the world into thinking that Kamit (Egypt) was a White or Semitic (mixed) country at the time the pyramids were built. Caucasians and Semites did eventually come into Kamit thousands of years after the pyramids were built. However, **the people in Egypt today** bear no more resemblance to Ancient Kamitans (Egyptians) than Caucasian people in America resemble Native Americans. No one would claim for instance that the majority of people you see in America today are the original people of this land. Obviously today's American population consists of the sons, and daughters of invaders and the sons, and daughters of those who either came here or were brought here during the great invasion. Likewise, The people who are in Kamit (Egypt) today are the sons, and daughters of invaders. That is, modern Arabs, not Native Kamitans.

The notion of **native Caucasian people of Africa is plain and simply a myth**. There is no scientific anthropological, or historic evidence to support such a claim. The White People in Azania (South Africa) are not native Africans. They are obviously the sons and daughters of European invaders. Despite the fact that they invented an African sounding name for themselves Afrikaans, no one would have any difficulty pointing out a European African from a Native African. The same is true in Kamit If you go to Kamit (Egypt) today and ask someone to point out a native Kamitan (Egyptian) they will point to an individual that looks like any other typical African. Strongly melaninated skin curly hair and African features. Don't let anyone sell you the White African Myth. If they do sell you the idea, be sure and ask about purchasing the Brooklyn Bridge,

Modern Movies and Museums have propagated the White African Myth. These two institutions have been among the biggest transmitters of

Mixed Egyptian AIDS. The fictional movie **Cleopatra** and other "religious" movies (Moses etc.) have depicted the people of Egypt and Canaan (Israel) as Caucasian. The only Black people in these movies were typically "slaves". This is contrary to what Afrikans, and historians of the time and the people of the time have reported as the ethnic reality of those particular areas[x]. Cleopatra, and that whole genre of ancient movies made in the west distort the image of Classical African Civilization. They dis-inform the viewer by mixing up truth with falsehood. They show accurate costumes and geographic, and architectural settings but misrepresent the ethnic mix of people. Putting the White myth spin on Kamit (Egypt) is like making a movie about Harlem (Black section of New York) and having the main characters and most of the actors cast as Caucasians singing and rapping hip hop.

Naturally the Harlem example is ludicrous. There are too many people alive today that know about the people and culture of Harlem. Therefore, trying to culturally poison people about Harlem culture is not likely to be successful. However, few people today know much about ancient Kamit (Egypt) and so it is relatively easy to culturally poison people about ancient African Culture.

Why is it that when you go into a museum like **the Metropolitan Museum of Art in New York** the "Egyptian" exhibit is nowhere near the African Exhibit? I am sure if you ask the good people of the museum why this is so; they would tell you that the structure of the building made it logical to keep the Egyptian exhibit away from the African exhibit or some other nonsense like that. I'm not picking on the Metropolitan. If you go to the **Boston Museum,** or other museums around the world you will find the same KO AIDS and "mixed Egyptian" AIDS game being played out. You need to understand that this is a deliberate attempt to culturally poison Americans about Classical African Civilization. The Kametic (Egyptian) exhibit should be connected to the rest of the African exhibit, in the same way that the Greek exhibit is connected to the European exhibits. Don't believe the hype!

The ancient **Kamitans (Egyptians) depicted themselves as Black.** As the inventors of recorded history, they made that fact a part of the historical record. This fact remained a historical, and archeological standard until the 15th century and the enslavement of Africans. Coincidentally, along with African enslavement came the invention and rise of racist scholarship. Martin Bernal in his book Black Athena volume [xi]one painstakingly worked out details of the invention of Mixed Egyptian AIDS, as well as the White Egyptian Myth. The "Aryan Model" over turned what he says in short is the original historical view of Kamit (Egypt) and Greece, which he calls the "Ancient Model". He names the people who invented this "Aryan Model" and the schools in Germany and later in France, England, and America that adapted this model as the standard model for teaching cultural history. With irrefutable scholarship he makes it plain, that the Aryan Model is a White supremacist model of cultural education that is still almost universally used in American schools. He proposes what he calls the Revised Ancient Model as a step aimed at returning the teaching of the classics in America to some semblance of reality. Understand that those college professors, and scholars known, as classicists are the most culturally poisoned group of individuals in America. As the so-called historical experts on European classical civilizations, they are the single largest group responsible for removing Classical African Civilization from American dictionaries, and history books. They have a large sophisticated tool bag of tricknology to infect Americans with various forms of cultural poisoning.

Mr. Bernal in Black Athena does an outstanding job of citing and foot noting the details so I will not try to repeat them here. Get the book. What I will do is provide you with the antidote (truth) to Mixed Egyptian AIDS, in the form of an ancient picture that is worth a thousand words. The following graphic shows first hand how the Kamitans saw and described themselves.

The Classical Ethnic Model

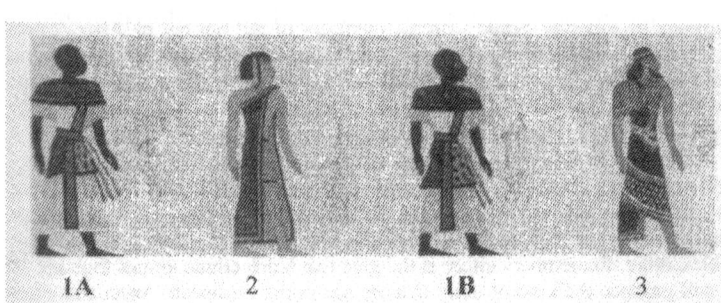

Figure 16 three ethnic groups

This Painting is from the tomb of Ramses III (1200 B.C.E.) It is one of many **Ethnographic studies** published by the (Egyptians). In producing the first such studies the Kamitians pictographicly described the three major ethnic groups. That is Africans Asians and Caucasians. They clearly depict themselves as being biologically the same as all other Africans.And distinct from Asians and Caucasians.

1A. The Kamitans as seen by themselves.
2. The Asian
1B. Other Africans
3.The Caucasian—Originally called Tambou by the Kamitans

In addition to the ethnograph, Egyptians left huge sculptures of themselves (statues, relief's etc.) in stone. Van Sertima in his book *Egypt Revisited* has done a photo essay of the great Kamitan (Egyptian) kings. From the sphinx (c.10, 000 B.C.E.[xii]) to the first king of the unified nation, Nemar to the famous king Tut, there is **no sign of the mythical White Africans.**[xiii] Historians are unanimous in their conclusion that Kametic (Egyptian) civilization was completely developed and all the pyramids completed before, the first non-Africans set foot on the continent in any significant numbers.

The Kamitans are primary sources for information about themselves. The secondary sources of that day confirm what the primary sources have said. That is Afrikans created Kamit and built the pyramids.

Secondary sources like the Greek and Roman historians, who visited the country in ancient times, even after the non -African invasions, also said the Kamitans were Black. Even the more removed sources like the Arabs, Moors and early European Renaissance historians during the time of Napoleon did not disagree with the primary and secondary sources regarding classical African civilization.

An example of a secondary source is Herodotus, the first great western historian who wrote nine books of history. He said that **all the people** from Kamit (Egypt) to India (**southern Asia) in his time were Black** (with dark skin and curly hair).

When you ask a western historian, or Egyptologist to explain how they refute this information they simply say their great historian Herodotus' information on Africa (Book II) can't be trusted because he was a little crazy and "unscientific". Yet the same people assert that the rest of his histories are ok and can be trusted. Is this type of response to be called scholarship? No. It is simply foolishness. . Again, when you look for the argument it is not that you find a weak or illogical argument, you literally find no real argument at all.

To summarize our discussion, not knowing the name or location of classical African civilization is a symptom of cultural poisoning, caused by African AIDS, and the two virulent strains Kamit out of Africa AIDS, and Mixed Egyptian AIDS. **The antidote is the primary sources**, the native people of Kamit (Egypt), their writings, ethnographs and stone statues.

So who is it that has perpetuated the White African myth? What is their agenda? This kind of cultural label does not help build team America. It is exactly this kind of disrespectful reverse psychological behavior that creates and insures disharmony in America. Some extreme members of the not out of Africa camp rather than acknowledge that, Afrikans built the pyramids have tried to imply that people from outer space built the pyramids. We all need to stop the foolishness. America can not expect to build a strong Team America with one hand, while she openly disrespects the cultures of fellow team members with the other hand.

If we as African Americans do not know and respect our classical culture, it is not logical to expect that other Americans would know and respect our ethnic group's long history and culture. The antidote for African cultural AIDS is to get to know your Classical African Civilization in the same way that European, and Asian Americans know their culture. Remember culture is the glue that holds ethnic groups together. It is, in fact, the only thing that will produce the kind of unity that we see in the European, Asian, and other American ethnic communities. The antidote for other Americans who are infected with one or all of the viruses noted is the same. Learn about your fellow countrymen's classical culture. If you are not inclined to read, and you know a culturally literate African American then ask him, or her, to tell you about their classical culture.

*   *   *

The Bigger Question: racism in education and attempted cultural genocide

Why are these dis-informative patterns so pervasive and what purposes do they serve? The thought of African people creating the first great civilization in the world is too damaging to the White supremacy belief system. Therefore, Anti-humanists have tried to poison the African cultural well. In the same way corporations try to gain market share for their product (have more people buy their product than the other company's product) there are educational forces in America that would try to gain mind share. That is getting you to buy their view of the world (Worldview product) instead of our own view. Don't believe the hype.

If we are to have an **honest discussion on race relations** in this country, all Americans must come to understand that our **institutions** in charge of teaching history have been **corrupted by** cultural poisoning. For years these institutions have been infecting Americans with dis-information, and misinformation about African culture which, is disrespectful to Africans and their descendents in America. I am not a historian, but like you I can read a map. We must demand that our so-called **"Qualified Historians" at least be able to get basic geography and biology right.** EGYPT IS IN AFRICA. AFRICANS BUILT THE PYRAMIDS AND CLASSICAL AFRIKAN CIVILIZATION.

4. Columbus

Did Columbus discover America? NO

Every one in the African American community **should know this by now**. How do you discover a place occupied by someone else? If my mate and I, approached you in your car and told you to get in the trunk because we have discovered your car we would be considered criminals, and you would probably have us arrested for theft. This, again, is a **case where people of color and Europeans seem to see two different truths**. Most Americans and indeed many people around the world still believe that Columbus did discover America. From the point of **view of the Native Americans**, African Americans or any other people of color, **Columbus's landing** in the Americas (Caribbean) **was a tragedy for mankind,** and was the initiating act of one of the world's worst physical and cultural genocidal processes.

80,000,000 Native Americans lived in the Americas in 1492.[xiv] By1592 there were only 10,000,000 Native Americans left alive. By 1990 there were only 1,878,285[xv] Native Americans left in the United States, that is a lot of human beings for Europeans to have murdered no matter how you measure it. The Jewish holocaust was 6 million; the African holocaust is estimated at 100,000,000 (middle passage/ WW0). **We don't celebrate the rise of Hitler** or the rise of the European enslavement trade or any other initiating act of physical and cultural genocide. **We should not celebrate** the initiating act of the **Native American genocide**. It is both immoral and disrespectful to those whose ancestors perished here.

To call Columbus an explorer or a settler from the Native American or African American perspective is to defy all logic and reason. His first acts in America were to capture and enslave human beings. He was by any standard a criminally insane anti-humanist. Untold numbers of criminally insane anti-humanists followed him to the Americas, and unjustly slaughtered tens of millions of Native Americans and stole their land. To call these people settlers is doublespeak.

To forget the realities cited above is what we call **Cowboy and Indian syndrome**. This syndrome was typified by the old T.V. westerns like the Long Ranger and Tonto. Generations of Americans grew up seeing these T.V. series and believing them to resemble reality. That is the cowboy as the good guy and the Native American as the bad guy. This is the opposite of what was the reality. The reality of that kind of thinking is a form of American romanticism. This syndrome is one of the forms of thought that creates American historic AIDS.

American historic AIDS (AH AIDS) is an information deficiency that causes most Americans to unrealistically romanticize the behavior of their ancestors. That is to tend to remember only the "good" things they did and conveniently forget the enormous harm they did to other human beings. AH AIDS is at the heart of the continuing American/Native American conflict. That is rather then realistically remembering, confronting and resolving the conflict Americans are comfortable taking the self serving route of forgetting about the criminal behavior perpetrated by America against Native Americans. American presidents and representatives have signed some 500 treaties as a form of making amends. Each one of these American promises has been broken. More then 400 of these treaties still are sitting in the congress of the United States swept under the American rug[xvi].

America has had a number of National **polices for dealing with Native Americans.** None of them were designed to produce harmonious relations between Native Americans and other Americans. All the policies in fact created just the opposite of harmony. The policies of **genocide, treaties and then termination** all produced harm, and justifiable hate and distrust on the part of Native Americans with regard to many other Americans. The possible exception to this series of anti Native American policies is the current casino policy, which at least allows for an income stream (untouched by the government) that can be put to good use by the Native Nations.

In talking about Columbus and the American Historic Aids it has produced, should help all Americans have a better grip on the reality of our past and present relationship with our fellow Native Americans. The romanticized Columbus myth is a symptom of America's cultural poisoning. Native Americans will tell you that America had an official policy of murdering their people (Genocide). The forked tongue of the treaty policy has already been discussed. And last but not least the termination policy, which actually lead to some Native American Nations voting to terminate themselves. (In effect saying lets not be Native American)

The continuation of the Columbus myth is a sign that all too many Americans still live in a sort of Historical Disney Land. Many still participate in Columbus Day parades, and some American sports teams still have Native American names and/or mascots. This is overtly disrespectful. These same "Americans" will then sit down at the National discussion on "race" table and proclaim their commitment to improving "race" relations. This is the height of moral hypocrisy. Native Americans and African Americans recognize that European American rhetoric does not match European deeds. European Americans can not maintain the position of arsonist and fireman at the same time on the "race" issue and expect to have any credibility with other ethnic groups.

*   *   *

Three final points that every American should know:

(1) In 1455 the Pope of the Catholic Church pronounced that the Native Americans were savages and did not have souls[xvii]. **The so-called "moral" leader of the European world sanctioned** the invasion of those people's land and the slaughtering of millions of innocent human beings.

That event marked the public acceptance of **wholesale murder**, partly sanctioned by religion's approval of the White supremacy philosophy/belief system. The first enslavement ship to force African prisoners of war to America was named the Jesus[xviii].

The European church and state sanctioned Columbus' invasion. Europeans invented economic, religious and scientific justifications for attacking other human beings and usurping their personal freedom and property. Those ungodly justifications combined with greed were used to dupe culturally illiterate Europeans and others into murderous behavior. The objective of raising this first point is to have you take note that the failure to identify and correct cultural poisoning (and Historic AIDS) with cultural literacy dooms a people to repeat the errors of the past. So later on in history we find Hitler using some of the same tactics to dupe "well educated" but culturally illiterate European Germans into murderous behavior.

(2) **African relations with Native Americans** for the most part were good. However, we were **not blameless in the Native American Holocaust**. Native Americans often took us into their nations to shield us from enslavement; we lived side by side with them in harmony. We often fought with them to protect their land (e.g. we held Florida with them for forty years against European invasion). Our ancestors were not on high moral ground when some became **"buffalo" soldiers** and killed Native Americans. We should feel sorrow and remorse for the misguided criminal actions of some of our ancestors in this regard. We should also publicly acknowledge and apologize for the evil behavior of our ancestors, in the same way that we would expect descendents of those who have perpetrated criminal actions against our ethnic group to do.

Cultural poisoning has had and continues to have a **profound effect on Native Americans and all other Americans.** Columbus said that he was looking for India and ran into America by "accident". According to the story he thought he was in India and therefore, called the people of the land "Indians". So either Columbus lied about whom he thought he saw here, or he was just stupid. In any case anyone who knows this story should also know that there are **no such people as "American Indians" (Amerindians).** There are Native Americans and this group of fictitious people that Columbus invented, Indians. One will note that culturally literate Native Americans refer to themselves by their normal national name for example Decota's, Algonquian's or simply as Native Americans which is the more, respectful term.

We can observe how profound the effects of cultural poisoning are by noting that, not only do European Americans use the fictitious term "American Indian" but also in the Native American Youth Conference, some Native Americans remarkably were still referring to themselves as "Indians". When America has tried to destroy a whole group of people, prevented them from practicing their religion (forcing them to convert to Christianity) or culture, lied to them (treaties) and tried to force them to terminate themselves, naturally those people would not be effective team players on "Team America". Americans can not both attack and disrespect other American ethnic groups, and complain that members of that group are not team players and are hostile.

In summary, European moral duplicity regarding Native Americans is not lost on other American ethnic groups. " Cowboy and Indian" syndrome creates American historic AIDS. The sub strain, Native American AIDS, has created culturally poisoned Native Americans, and Americans in general. The Native American/American conflict is the first American conflict, and must not only be included in the national discussion on "race", it must be understood as a critical part of the discussion on "race". Because the cure for this first American conflict is the same process needed to resolve America's latter, and sometimes more visible ethnic conflicts.

Lastly on this topic, everyone should know that not only did Columbus not discover anything, He was not even the first to visit the Americas from another continent. **Africans were here long before Columbus.**

*   *   *

The Bigger Question: Who was here before Columbus?
(Something to think about)

Our historians know who came to the Americas and when and where they settled[xix]. Why is this not mentioned in our schools? You need to find out who was here if you are really interested in keeping it real. The historic record indicates that Africans **came as teachers and builders** not as "slaves" or murderers in the eleventh century before Columbus was even born.

How would the view of African Americans be different if the first landing of Africans in the Americas as free world citizens, and as African nationals was common knowledge, as opposed to Americans just knowing about the second landing of Africans as prisoners of war (enslaved human beings)? How would our view of the second landing of European Americans (Vikings were the 1st landing) change if that landing was put in its proper historical sequence and context?

Lets take **a snap shot off our progress with the CP Test**. In the first two questions we demonstrated that cultural poisoning exists in the western worldview. We use the examples of the Peters map, and the European Continental Myth to illustrate that fact. In the third question, we demonstrated that CP has attempted to make Classical African Civilization disappear from the minds of men.

In the **fourth question,** we demonstrated that CP infects Americans even regarding the history of the land we occupy. We illustrated the general concept of American Historical AIDS, and the specific disorder of Native American AIDS.

The point is, not only is it possible to Culturally Poison folks about ancient or foreign cultures, and history. But Cultural Poisoning is also very effective up close and personal. So CP effects American recent and continuing history right here at home. Yes Cultural Poisoning can corrupt our national view of ourselves historically.

In the **fifth and next question** we will stay in America and look at another modern form of American Historical AIDS. Specifically we will be discussing George Washington, and the moral baggage connected with so called American heroes.

5. George Washington

Was President George Washington a hero to all Americans? No

George Washington is not a hero to African Americans who know that he enslaved their ancestors. He is not a hero to American humanists in general who find his criminal behavior against Africans reprehensible. Humanists would no more present Washington as a hero to African Americans, than they would present Hitler as a hero to Jewish Americans.

Who would find Washington as a hero? Anti humanists consider him as a hero, for they see African enslavement as having been no big deal, and maybe even a natural state of affairs. There is also, a large segment of culturally poisoned American humanists who do not understand it as a problem.

So the Question that many Americans are discussing in this new age of cultural enlightenment is. "Who of America's traditional heroes should accurately be called heroes, and who should simply be presented as notable men, and women in our history?"

George Washington had a **mixed history of good and bad behavior,** with respect to his dealings with his fellow human beings.

Washington from a European American point of view was **the father of the country.** He gained this title, and hero status as leader of the continental army that defeated the British, and gained independence for the nation. Washington was a key member of the "founding fathers" who created the constitution, which became the law of the land. He was also the first President of the United States (1789[xx]). The American romantic view of Washington contains stories that imply that he was honest to a fault. For example, as the legend goes, he admitted to his father that he cut down the Cherry tree stating that "he could not tell a lie."

On the flip side of his historical and moral ledger he is revealed to have been the worst type of anti-humanist. He was a racist, and an enslaver of his fellow men. He had upwards of 200 enslaved Africans. In 1776 he sent one of his slaves, to be exchanged for molasses.[xxi] Despite the fact that Crispus Attucks (African American) was the first American, to give his life for American independence, Washington, on April 28th 1775, declared that he did not want Blacks to fight for the colonies. Fellow racists, Benjamin Franklin and John Hancock agreed with Washington.[xxii] Only when America was losing the war did they decide they needed African Americans in the war. He wrote Colonel Henry Lee, December 10, 1775 "Success will depend on which side can arm the Negro faster"[xxiii]

Last but not least, **Washington actually raped African females he enslaved.** He, like many of the "founding fathers", fathered a number of mixed children. Many descendents of those anti-humanists are around today to name those criminals in their family tree. To name just a few, Patrick Henry of "give me liberty or give me death" fame was a rapist as was Thomas Jefferson. Jefferson had many mixed children as a result of his raping of adolescent African girls. That pedophile was notorious for not letting his children go to school. At the age of ten he had them working all day.[xxiv] And it is interesting to note that today, these so-called morally righteous republicans, are chasing President Clinton around about legal sex. Clinton is actually a Boy Scout compared to the "heroes" of those very same Republicans.

America is not suffering from some new moral rot. American Presidents have suffered from moral turpitude since the inception of this nation. The immoral behavior of Mr. Starr and the take no prisoners, get Clinton at any cost, Republican jihad is a far greater crime against the constitution than Clinton's sexual indiscretion. Social conservative republicans, are correct when they say our President should have high moral standards. However, what about their own moral behavior? Is unjustifiably threatening and coercing witnesses with various forms of legal force, and setting perjury traps based on illegitimate questions about an American citizens personal sexual behavior, moral behavior? No, it is immoral legal slight of hand.

*   *   *

Many Republicans hate President Clinton. Why? In our "civil" society we often disagree with a Presidents policies, or we may even dislike him personally, hating however, is not supposed to be part of our political equation. So why has this been the case with President Clinton?

Lets look more closely at **the Republican Party**. They are made up of economic and social conservatives. It is my opinion, that most of the racists from the Democratic Party have left the party and gone over to the Republicans, and now call themselves by the politically correct (doublespeak) title of "social conservatives". They are lead by individuals that have made it clear that they believe that this is a "White" Christian country destined to be governed by "White" Christians.

What has Clinton done to warrant their hate? Well first he openly has African American friends like Vernon Jordan. He says proudly that he has appointed more African Americans to government posts than any President in the history of America. He has started a National Discussion on "race". By the way incase you haven't noticed, we do not hear social conservatives saying that they are in favor of such a discussion in our Nation. And last but not least, he has had the unmitigated gall to make an official presidential trip to Africa, and say that "Europeans... were wrong for enslaving Africans".

This President grew up during the civil rights movement, and the immoral Vietnam War. His 21st century **multi-ethnic approach to American government** has made him a hated man among anti-humanist social conservatives. Many regard him as a cultural criminal bent on destroying "White" Christian culture in America. It is not Clinton's sexual behavior that has gotten him in trouble with American anti-humanists, but his cultural behavior. Anti-humanist hatred, and misguided Republican humanists, have focused their energy around articles of impeachment and/or actual impeachment despite 60 to 75% of the American public saying that they do not want this nations last democratic presidential election to be reversed (no impeachment).

The question has been asked **why are African Americans Clinton's most loyal supporters** at the 85-95% approval level? The answer is simple. African Americans are in a unique position to recognize unfairness, and injustice when they see it in America. World leaders, and world citizens also recognize anti-humanists behavior as demonstrated by the standing ovation President Clinton received at the United Nations, just after Mr. Starr's four hour porno video dump. Unlike Newt, real world leaders like Nelson Mandella, standing on the high moral ground renew their support, and friendship for President Clinton. The support for Clinton by the American public in general and African Americans in particular is not because the masses are asses, but because the masses have glasses. And they don't see the second governmental shutdown by the Republican jihad as productive for America.

I jumped **from George Washington to Clinton to make the point,** that this discussion of Washington is not an irrelevant discussion about dead presidents from the past. Quite to the contrary, it is a contemporary discussion about truth and morality, questions our nation continues to struggle with to this very day. Anti-humanist are able to paralyze the government (legislative gridlock) and palm off this national discussion on sex, on the American people by taking advantage of the reality that most Americans suffer from American Historic AIDS.

As we return to our discussion regarding our friends, "honest" Washington, and the founding fathers, let us not loose sight of the moral of the Clinton/Lewinsky show. This made for TV "political circus" orchestrated by social conservatives (mind you) is not an indication of a new moral rot in America, but, rather a warning that traditional American moral double standards are getting harder to sweep under the political rug. Americans are thinking more critically about who their hero's ought and ought not to be. From dead presidents to living ones, few have been able to claim the high moral ground. If we continue to lie to ourselves about the past, we can not expect to get too much truth out of the present or the future.

If you have ever wondered whether it is **better to tell the truth** or tell a lie, all you have to do today to get an answer is turn on your TV. Lack of truthfulness can create quite a national and personal mess. Truth is always the best policy, whether one is talking about the past or the present.

Finally, **speaking about the truth,** we can not forget that George was one of the "founding fathers" who legislated hard working African Americans as 3/5 of a Human being. George Washington's false hero status is an image that can be compared to most of the other "founding fathers". These people while notable figures in our history were also in part criminally insane. They were responsible directly and indirectly for the enslavement, and murder of other human beings. They raped women, and fathered a number of "illegitimate" children. Failure to remember the criminal behavior of Washington and his ilk is a sub-strain of **American Historical AIDS** we call **Hero AIDS**. It leaves many Americans in the excessively romantic culturally poisoned state of false hero worship.

It is an outrage that some Americans would insist that African Americans consider these individuals to be heroes. Any African, who had killed the enslaver, George Washington would rightfully be considered a hero today by African Americans. More and more thinking African Americans want the names of public schools, largely attended by African American children, changed from Washington High to something less insulting. This is a good sign that Cultural Poisoning is on the decline in some areas of America.

Holding up George Washington and the confederate flag[xxv] as symbols of American heroism is disrespectful to African Americans. Any American who is interested in forming Team America, should not tolerate this. You do not form a team by insulting your fellow players. Those who do insist on disrespecting team members should be ejected from the playing field, and made to sit on the bench until their human skills improve. George Washington is definitely not a hero to all Americans.

*   *   *

The Bigger Question: What kind of image do you have of America

That is **do you have a realistic image of America** and your American ancestors? Or do you have the one-sided romantic American image that George Washington represents? Having the realistic image is positive for Team America. Having the romantic image is counterproductive to the formation of Team America.

It is no wonder **Americans are not clear on this question**. Our "Public" schools (Some call them government schools) for the most part still tell the romantic version of the Washington myth. African Americans who have visited his home in Mt Vernon tell us the tour guides still tell the romantic story to visitors. This debate could easily be put to rest if Americans were interested in the truth. A simple DNA test of Washington's remains compared to his living mixed descendents would resolve the issue once and for all.

It is not that we in American can not find the truth. In America's first 400 years we seem not to be looking for it.

In fact, we seem to have at least one national ritual of lying. Remember Christmas and Santa Clause. If we start out lying to our young children what are we teaching them about the truth. Is it any wonder we Americans end up not looking for the truth given how we started out?

Now in the smaller question, I jumped from George to Clinton as a modern president because, Clinton's lack of truth can be funny when it is not sad and all too common among men, and woman here in America. I could have jumped from George to Johnson and the Vietnam War. But, there is nothing funny about war. A Government does not build Team America when it kills its children and lies about it.

*   *   *

Two final "food for thought" items. All Americans should **understand the contribution of African American ancestors to this nation**. African Americans in the 18th century were the hardest working people in this country. They worked from sun up to sun down for no pay, and fought to help get this country its independence from Europe. Africans were this country's source of wealth, and the country would be a far different place without their input. African Americans have been, and are one of America's greatest assets.

European American ancestors started this nation in both good and bad directions. We need to realistically understand, admit to and correct the wrong direction so we do not keep heading down unproductive roads of untruth.

So, George Washington is not a hero, but the bigger question is Truth in America, and what are we going to do about it.

Let's take **a snap shot of our progress with the CP Test**. In the first two questions, we demonstrated that cultural poisoning exist in the western worldview. We use the examples of the Peters map, and the European continental myth. In the third, fourth, and fifth questions we have looked at how cultural poisoning has effected our view of African Americans, Native Americans, our history, and our heroes.

In the sixth question regarding "Jesus Christ" we will look at how Cultural Poisoning has affected our spiritual/religious views. That is, how we see the world or cosmos as a general proposition.

6. Jesus Christ?

Are the popular Western pictures of Jesus Christ consistent with his physical description in the Holy Bible? NO

If you are not already aware, we will point out to you why the popular pictures of a European Jesus, we so often see in America, are not consistent with the description of Jesus in the King James Version of the Holy Bible. This is not a religious book, and the point of this question is not to tell anyone that one religion is better than another one. The point of this question like all the other questions is to **point out specific instances where cultural poisoning has corrupted something, in this case the practice of religion**. That is to say, in the same way that CP has corrupted our view of the world, and of various ethnic groups it has corrupted our spiritual views. We are asking you to critically think about your ideas, and beliefs regarding spirituality (religion). Compare your ideas with the instances of what we call **religious AIDS,** and determine for yourself whether or not, cultural poisoning has corrupted your spiritual views.

It never ceases to amaze me, the number of people including some ministers, who refer to the biblical person Jesus as **Jesus Christ as if that was his first and last name.** If you don't already know, Christ was a title meaning the anointed one, and was actually given to many people of that time (tax collectors and people from many walks of life). In the ancient tradition the title Christ, or the Anointed one, was given to those who were considered to be spiritually developed. Now understand, that I did not say that there was no such person as Jesus. What I said is that there was no person with the first name of Jesus, and a last name of "Christ". The correct phrasing of the two terms is Jesus the Christ. The reason for pointing out **Jesus Christ AIDS,** is to illustrate to the reader, that a Christian with this particular information deficiency. Either has it because his church failed to give him the proper context for the use of the two words, or in fact gave him inaccurate information, in telling him or inferring that Christ was Jesus' last name. So the first point we want to make, is that the Christian Church can by omission or commission provide its members with less than full and accurate information regarding their beliefs.

If something so basic as the correct biblical name, and title for the Son of God can be misrepresented then **we should be cautious when we read the bible.** One should be clear on whether we are reading **history, allegory, or mythology** in the bible. For instance, when we talk about history we are talking about factual things, or events in history that actually happened as opposed to allegory or mythology which may or may not represent historical facts. **The nativity scene** (Jesus in the manger) could be read as a historical event. We often see replicas of this scene at Christmas time here in America. Often this scene has snow everywhere. Now it is 110 degrees in the shade in that part of the world so there was definitely no snow. Since we have snow at Christmas this may be understandable, but it is never the less a misrepresentation of the historical facts. Where there is smoke there is fire. Where there is snow there are Caucasians. How many children have grown up thinking that it is entirely natural, and accurate to have both snow, and Caucasians in that part of the world? With out the benefit of critical thinking it is all too short a leap from one misrepresented fact to other false conclusions or inferences.

If historical facts like the name of the Son of God, and his birth can be misrepresented, then it should not surprise you that **Jesus' ethnicity may have been misrepresented.** I grew up as a practicing Catholic Christian. My mother was from the Caribbean, and grew up as a Christian. I was taught at home, and in church that the bible was the indisputable word of God, and that all that was in the bible was true, and to be believed with out question. For proof of any thing related to Jesus one only needed to look to the bible with faith.

The Bible says he had hair like lambs wool and feet like brass burnt in an oven[xxvi]. You don't need to be a religious scholar, to decipher this description as more closely describing a strongly melaninated African than a European. As a Christian this was all the evidence I needed. Case closed.

*   *   *

If I was not a Christian and wanted to **go beyond the Bible's historical description** of Jesus' ethnicity for external confirmation where would I go? Well, I could look at the ethnicity of **his parents**. And I could inquire about the ethnicity of the **people of his time,** and what ethnicity they thought him to be. Finally what did **the founding fathers** of the Christian church agree that his ethnicity was? What would these four inquiries tell me? Would they tend to confirm or refute the authority of the bible?

1. **What was the ethnicity of Jesus' mother**? The original Madonna, and child statues were of an **African Mother and African child,**[xxvii] Auset and Heru (the Greek Isis and Horus), before the Christian iconoclasm (distorting and destroying of African statues and religious works). Historian Will Durant says, " Statues of Isis and Horus were renamed Mary and Jesus[xxviii]" This would not have been possible unless, Jesus and his mother were known to be Black by most people of the time. The early Madonna's of the Christian church were black until the time of the European renaissance.[xxix] Tradition holds that St Luke who knew Jesus' mother personally carved Black statues of her. There are Black Madonna's in France, Switzerland, Italy, Spain, Russia and many other locations in Europe. The English scholar, Jocelyn Rhys says there are statues of Black virgins from early Christian worship in the catacombs of Rome. Life Magazine ran a story with a picture of the Pope worshiping a Black Madonna in his private chapel. These are all obviously summary bottom line statements from larger works[xxx]. You will note they all point in the same direction. Jesus' Mother was Black. Don't take my word for it, look it up for your self.

2. **What ethnicity were the people of the land**? Most of us watched the Persian Gulf war on T.V. You will recall that it was 110 degrees in the

shade. The **native people of that land were Africans.** Science tells us through "**Gloger's Law**[xxxi]," which applies to both animals, and man that mammals born and evolved in this type of climate always have dark pigmented skin. The Greeks, and Romans of the time referred to the natives of Canaan (Israel) as Ethiopians (people of burnt faces)[xxxii]. So we can conclude that people of the time were generally melaninated. I can recall nothing in the bible that indicated that, Jesus was ethnically different from most native people in the land of the bible (Palestine-thin strip of land-between North Africa and Arabia)

3. What ethnicity was Jesus? The Madonna information provided above gave us the answer before we even got to the direct question. However, there is additional even more direct evidence. There is graphic hard evidence that instructs us that, most of the people of that time believed that Jesus' appearance was consistent with his description in the bible. **The Jesus coin:** In the British Museum there is a coin of Justinian II[xxxiii]. On the front is Justinian, on the back of the coin is Jesus the Christ,

Figure 17 Jesus Coin

with tightly curled hair. The Cambridge Encyclopedia says: " Whatever the fact, this coin places beyond a doubt the belief that Jesus Christ was a Negro."[xxxiv]

4. What do the church fathers have to say on the matter? I started by giving you the biblical authority for Jesus' ethnicity rev. 1.14. The founding father's canonized (agree on what should and should not be in it) the bible. Therefore, we must conclude that they also agreed on the descriptions of Jesus, that they included in the canonized works of the bible

So **where does this information lead our thinking** regarding the question posed? The bible contains a clear description of Jesus' ethnicity, and there is a substantial body of confirming evidence. However, this is not what the catholic or most other Christian religions teach about the historicity of Jesus and his times. The obvious question is why?

Based on the information provided **we can now answer the question** with one word "religious AIDS". If we want to be more informative, we can use two concise sentences. The cultural virus **religious AIDS** causes many Christian leaders, and followers to be culturally poisoned. This poisoning leads them astray from the description in the bible, and the evidence on the ground causing the production of corrupted religious information.

*   *   *

From the early days of the African Christian church in the city of Alexandria in Egypt, the European church has gone through **various phases of Europeanizing their church**. The phase that effects us most here in America is the European renaissance phase. During this time a homosexual psychologically disturbed European[xxxv] by the name of Michael Angelo painted biblical scenes on the ceiling of the Sistine chapel. He obviously disregarded biblical descriptions like Rev.1.14 and painted them in the image of his own ethnic group. While this is understandable, we must also understand that Michael Angelo's interpretation is inconsistent with the bible, and the other facts cited. The pictures in the **Sistine Chapel** have been the **models for most of the images of Jesus** we see here in America today. Often the picture we see in churches, and books is a copy of Jesus as painted in the Sistine Chapel. So specifically, who is it in the picture that has represented Jesus to so many Americans?

On a number of occasions, I have been told that **Michael Angelo's diary** contains the answer. What I have been told goes as follows. We have Michael Angelo's writings, where he tells us which European people he used as models to paint the religious figures on the ceiling if the Sistine chapel. He wrote that **his cousin was the model for Jesus**. Now to be clear, I have not checked this out for myself, so I can not personally claim it to be the case with certitude however, it does sound plausible. This is the closest I can come at this point to answering the question of who's in the picture if it isn't Jesus? For those who have asked me this question, the important thing to note (whether or not the picture is of his cousin) is that the picture doesn't fit the melaninated description in the bible.

I brought up the Michael Angelo's cousin issue, to make the point that some things we think we know; (I use to worship this picture in my mother's house) may not only be untrue. But may be so far from the truth that you just may wind up worshiping some guy's cousin. **When it comes to religion be especially careful** about what you are told, and what you believe. Check it out for your self, including this cousin thing.

We will end this question where we started. It was not my intent to imply that one religion is better than another, or to imply that Christianity has no value. All the major religions and their great books have value. It was my intent to point out where cultural poisoning has corrupted the teaching of one of the major religions. No doubt there is corruption in other religions like Islam, Judaism, The book of Mormon, etc. I covered the more obvious corrupted information of Christianity, because I was raised as a Christian and have some familiarity with that religious institution.

Far more important than the specific issue of Jesus' ethnicity is a more general question. How is it we seem to know more about our jobs, (temporary salvation) then we do about our spiritual development (eternal salvation)? As we move to eradicate cultural poisoning in every aspect of human endeavor, you should understand that spirituality plays an indispensable role. Our spiritual orientation and moral bent, has everything to do with our capacity to reduce Cultural Poisoning. Understanding this lets move on the bigger spiritual image question.

*   *   *

The bigger Question: What spiritual images do you have?

Whether you consider yourself a religious person or not American religion has played a role in your degree of cultural poisoning. This is true for all Americans, but especially true if you are an African American. How has corrupt religious information been used here in America to create ethnic conflict? First Africans had their own religions in their Nation of domicile before being attacked by Europeans, and being brought to America as prisoners of war. Once here, European tricknology, and the threat of violence forced them to give up their religions, and take on the worship of a White Son of God. This was done for a purpose. When you see the Son of God you see the father. It would have been hard to revolt against people who looked like God. Some Africans, in this culturally poisoned state, came to believe it was the natural order of things for the people that looked like god to control their lives.

Christianity in the early days was a religion with large percentages of its members going to **church on Sunday and killing African Americans or Native Americans on Monday.** The god that the European Columbus worshiped, and the God that the Native Americans prayed to were apparently two different Gods. The reality is that early European American Christian institutions are a prime example of culturally poisoned "religious" practice. These institutions were so completely corrupted by the White supremacy belief system to be rendered almost completely useless as "religious" institutions.

I do not say this with malice or to be disrespectful. I'm simply illustrating what's true, or at least what is obviously not true. It is simply not true to say that the European image of Jesus is consistent with Jesus' description in the bible.

It has been said, that **black people speak Black using English.** I believe that the same can be said about the religion we practice. African Americans practice African spirituality using modern religion. One need only visit a Catholic Church on Sunday morning and then visit a Baptist

Church. It will become immediately apparent—even to the non-religious—that a different spirit is active in the two different ceremonies and congregations. What kind of spirit do you have? What are the elements that make up the human spirit? Isn't it interesting that we seem to **know, more about our jobs then we do about our spirit?**

Any thinking person **should be suspect of historical Sunday/ Monday organizations.** That is to say organizations whose members, and leaders were known to go to church on Sunday, and kill Africans or Native Americans (or any body else) on Monday.

Not only are their two America's there are two Christian religions in America. Historically you should be aware that in early America, African Americans were not permitted to worship in European American Christian churches. Not only was the African forced to believe in Christianity as mentioned earlier but, Africans were forced to worship separate from other Americans. This might be called the European American **doctrine of separate but equal gods.** Think for a minute about the ungodly hypocrisy of such a doctrine.

Today we still find that the majority of African Americans go to predominantly African American churches. And the same can be said for European Americans. On the intolerant side of the religious chessboard, we see the resurgence of the conservative religious right. On the tolerant side of the religious chessboard, we see an increase in multi-ethnic religious institutions. This last development is good for Team America.

What is important to note here is that if a person is culturally poisoned, he is **not automatically cured when he becomes a minister,** or a priest, or a Christian. If a person is an anti-humanist, racist, or a Cultural Terrorist, he or she does not lose this mental disorder when they become a police person, or a minister, or priest, or a Christian. So the leadership of a religious institution can corrupt the practice of religion, and use religion to spread cultural poisoning. It is this lack of telling the truth that has caused the great decline in membership in many American religious institutions of all ethnic groups. The greatest decline has been among the nations youth. Most of the hip-hop generation, for example, (while many still believe in god) literally think of the church as a big joke.

In an effort to realigning their spiritual orientation or help to make their churches more culturally relevant, I am happy to say that many Americans are not standing still on the spiritual issues of America. They are thinking about the issue, and taking action, regarding religious institutions infected with moral turpitude. Their actions in the main have taken one of two forms. **One form of action** has been making Christian **institutions less culturally poisoned,** and more culturally literate. In the African American community we can see the cultural movement with ministers, for example, wearing African material, or artifacts indicating that they no longer accept the premises that their cultural orientation, and spiritual orientation should be entirely separate. This is a good thing, and makes their religious experience more culturally relevant. In the European American community the multi-ethnic movement is a positive action.

*   *   *

The other action being taken by Americans in significant numbers is the realigning of their spiritual orientation, altogether **away from traditional American Christianity,** and toward other spiritual systems. Some (especially African American youth) have turned to Islam, and countless others have moved toward Asian spiritual systems like Yoga or Transcendental Meditation, etc.

As you think about your spirituality **which of the two types of action are you inclined to take?** Naturally the choice is a personal one. If you are **taking action one,** that is staying in your religious group and reducing Cultural Poisoning. You need to ask yourself the following questions. If you go to church does your church spread culturally poisoned information or cultural literacy? If your church needs to be more culturally literate can you help it get there? Then you need to make that effort if you plan to stay associated with that institution. If your own literacy is not at the level it needs to be for you to be of assistance in this regard, you need to get it there.

When taking action two, switching religious institutions, or systems the process you should follow is less obvious. The range of choices is enormous including **do it yourself** spirituality. That means not connecting to any particular institution, but managing your own spiritual development. What you decide obviously depends on what you're looking for. The best I can tell most Americans thinking about the switch action is, narrow your options based on what you expect to learn from you spiritual (religious) relationship. There is one group of Americans I would like to give some more specific advice and that's my own group, African Americans.

If you are an African American and planning to switch, you have an additional set of choices you may not have even thought about, the African spiritual traditions. Yes that's right. Just as there are European religions, and Asian religions there are African "religions". While most Africans were forced to give up their spiritual systems, not all did. And many of the descendants of those forces away from their spiritual traditions have returned to an African spiritual system. These systems are practiced all over America in most major cities. The systems range form **Santeria to Yoruba to the Ausar Auset Society**[xxxvi]. If for instance your criterion for a suitable spiritual system includes, a physical and spiritual component, you may be considering Ti-Chi or YOGA. If you are considering YOGA, religious AIDS may prevent you from being aware of all the information you need to make an informed decision. For example, did you know that there is a discipline called African YOGA? While the Asian ethnic group is most widely known for the practice of YOGA in modern times, YOGA originated in Africa. It came into Asia though India (once called little Africa). **African "YOKA"** is commonly practiced in America under the title Egyptian YOGA[xxxvii]. If you don't know where to find these groups go to your local African American book store, or get an African American news paper. Look in the yellow pages, or talk to a culturally literate friend. You need to consider all your options in order to make the most informed judgment.

What spiritual image do you have running in your bio-computer, and how does that image effect your self image, and that of your ethnic group? Do you have Micheal Angelo's cousin's picture in the church you attend, or in your bedroom? Why? Has cultural poisoning caused you to abandon your ethnic spirituality, and believe that the Son of God or God is European? Who did your ancestors worship, or do you believe they were superstitious ignorant savages with no religion of value? Who told you they had no religion? Why do you think it was important to prevent enslaved human beings from reading or practicing their own religion?

Spirituality (religion) is the most difficult subject to think about, that is why it, along with politics is seldom talked about in polite conversation. We are past the time for polite conversation in America. We need to have some bottom line discussions with ourselves and with each other. I raised more questions than answers, because only you have your own spiritual answers. Hopefully, we have asked you the right questions to help you think about who you are, how you relate to your god, yourself, other men and the cosmos.

CP test snap shot: at this point we have looked at how cultural poisoning has effected Western, Asian and African worldviews. In this last question we have discussed how CP has effected your spiritual view. In question seven we will next discuss how CP may have effected your personal image (view) of yourself.

7. Good Hair

Do you, a member of your family or a friend of yours have good hair? NO (That is, would you agree that straight or curly hair is more desirable than "kinky" hair?)

No, there is no such thing as good hair. This belief that there is good, and bad hair is an **example of** a form of **cultural poisoning** known as **image poisoning** that still plagues most people of color to this very day.

For non-African Americans who are reading at this point, you are probably wondering what I am talking about. You should know that most **African American and Latino American readers** understand exactly what I mean. This "bad hair" syndrome, from my observation, is restricted to our respective communities. European Americans do not have a "bad" hair myth in the same sense that I am referring to it here. For instance, we would find it odd if we looked back in history, and found a point in time where a significant percentage of Europeans suddenly believed that their hair was "bad" and decided, to make it look more like African hair.

Let me take a stab at clearing up **the bad hair myth.** The type of hair that a people have is **biologically produced naturally and relative to the climate** in which they developed. **Africans** have tightly curled hair, not kinky, and not nappy. Curly hair has air pockets that help keep the brain cool in hot, or tropical climates. **"White" people** (the name they gave themselves), typically have longer, straight hair. Straight hair serves as a mat to keep the head warm in cold climates. **This does not make white hair or " white—like" hair "good," just different.**

If you came to this continent naturally thinking that your hair was good curly hair like all the people you lived with, **who tricked you** into thinking the opposite? How did you get the idea (belief) that someone else's hair is good, or better than yours is?

If your hair (black hair) **is not what is referred to as "good", then what does that make it** then? "Bad hair", something less than good hair? It should be obvious that this type of **labeling could not be good for your self-esteem.** Further, if your belief in the notion of good hair is not based on what is functional but on your idea of what is considered to be beautiful, then **what standard do you use to measure beauty**? White people? Why? What about your own ethnic group's standard for beauty?

What is your good hair belief based on? There are **three things** it could be based on, hair **function, beauty,** or **nothing at all**. By nothing I mean **"you heard it from somebody"** or "every one you know uses the term good hair". If this is the reason you believe in the **good hair myth,** it is the equivalent to **having no reason at all**. That is, you have heard something, and **failed to check to see if it is true**.

Hair function is a biological fact. **If your belief in good hair is based on biology** instead of some externally imposed standard of beauty, then you need to understand, that African hair has a high melanin content which protects it from the sun's UV rays. In this same way, melanin protects our skin and eyes. From a biological perspective if you live in a tropical, or sunny climate, **then Black (African) hair should be considered "good hair",** because it is biologically designed to be most effective in that climate.

White hair, blond hair in particular (which is considered the "best"), **has less melanin and is less protected** from the sun. If a Caucasians hair is long and straight then it is good protection in cold climates.

However, it is less then biologically ideal for hot climates. You have seen the discoloration, or burning (bleaching) of European hair as a result of exposure to the sun. **If your hair were to burn up when you went outside** would you then classify it as "good hair"? Of course not! This simply illustrates the absurdity of one pervasive misconception that helps contribute to psychologically poisoning African Americans about their self-image. It is a form of cultural poisoning we call image poisoning.

Finally, my research indicates that at least **75% of African Americans have been affected,** or infected by this particular distortion of reality. The good hair myth is part of image AIDS.

My recommendation in the case of the good hair question is if you suffer from this element of cultural image poisoning fix it. If you run into another brother, or sister who suffers from it then help them fix it.

If you are Black and based your belief on nothing, then you'd better start basing your beliefs on something. You should be asking yourself, **"what other beliefs do I hold about my self image that are not based on anything?"** And "what am I going to do about it?"

If you are White and you believe you have good hair, and black people have bad hair, how did you get this notion, and what is it based on? Do you think some ethnic groups are less attractive, or ugly (hair being part of this judgment) and if so, how does this effect your actions, and reactions to these people? You should understand that African Americans are not unaware of the beliefs held by their fellow countrymen. We see it on TV every day. Now everyone is entitled to his, or her own opinion. It has been said that beauty is in the eye of the beholder. However, the **ethno-phobic** elements of beauty standards go beyond the simple "eye of the beholder" theory. African Americans should know there is no such reality as "good hair". Forget about that concept. It is destructive to your self-image.

*   *   *

The Bigger Question: Image Poisoning

If you are African American, hair is only one aspect of one's self image. What other ideas do you hold that are poisonous to your image? What about light skin, and dark skin? Which do you prefer? Why? What other questions should you be asking your self? The "good" hair myth is both a personal image poisoning issue, and a group poisoning issue. That is what you think about yourself effects how you think about your group. If you hate yourself there is a good chance you will project this self-hatred onto you ethnic group. We have all heard the stories of the brother who steps on another brother's sneakers, and gets punched or shot for his perceived disrespect. What is that about? It is about the same thing, self-hatred.

If you are a European American TV executive, and tend to put mainly light skinned African Americans on T.V., are you engaged in culturally poisoned behavior? Would you say that this particular form of xenophobic behavior has helped, or harmed inter-ethnic harmony in America? What could you do to present ethnic American images in a way that would cause Americans to be more open, and prepared to play on Team America?

Image poisoning is one of the most insidious, and dangerous forms of cultural poisoning. It effects everything else that a person does, from family relationships, to educational goals, to job possibilities. When this type of poisoning is present it is deep seated and has usually started in childhood, and may now be below the adult's consciousness.

Americans should all be aware of the **psychological test conducted by the NAACP** during the civil rights battles of the 1960's. The Thurgood Marshall movie now shown on T.V. replicates the testing of African American children in the south. The children were shown a Black, and a White doll. They were then asked questions like which doll was smarter, more honest, handsomer etc. the Black children invariably chose the White doll. The look on the faces of these culturally poisoned children, when asked, "which doll are you?" was unforgettable. Cultural Poisoning, and its effect on ones self image, is not just an intellectual exercise it has serious real world consequences. It is a deep-seated psychological disorder, and operates similarly to an addiction. The first step in the recovery process is the same as for the alcoholic, one must first admit that he has the disease before the healing process can begin. Hopefully, one of the reasons you are taking the cultural poisoning self-test is to do some self-assessment about how you see yourself, and your ethic group. In your process don't underestimate the importance of this question despite the fact that we started out simply talking about the seemingly trivial subject of hair. **There is a shorter distance from hair to skin color than you think!**

*   *   *

Self-assessment is never easy. Of all the types of assessment one might perform self-assessment is the most difficult. It is always easy to find fault in others, but very difficult to see it in one's self. In the case of image poisoning, and the resulting cultural poisoning, the task has been especially difficult for Americans, because there has been no specific language, or set of words one could use to look at personal CP. One of the important tasks of The Cultural literacy strategy is to provide some of those words. To be effective at Cultural self—assessment first one must admit that he, or she may be infected with CP. The next step is carefully listening on a daily basis to the words you use to describe yourself. That is both the words you use aloud, and the internal words you use in the privacy of your mind.

For our youth, if you use the word "nigger" to describe your self, you must recognize that that is a symptom of self image poisoning. (Image AIDS). If you call your woman the following names, or if you are a woman, and call yourself the following names you are exhibiting symptoms of cultural poisoning; Bitch, Ho, Bum Bitch, etc.

For adults, the symptoms most likely are not as obvious, and will require more careful listening. If you are an African American (of African decent) and you think of yourself, just as an American and get angry, or insulted when someone puts "African" in front of your American title, then you need to recognize this as a CP symptom. If you are having trouble with looking at your self, and you have kids how you interact with your children can give you some clues to the programs running in your bio-computer. Do you favor light skinned children, over dark skinned children? Do you call, or think of your children as, nasty or ugly? If someone asked you the question "what do your children think about "race" do you answer, "I don't know we have never talked about it?" If you are an

African American you are exhibiting a symptom. If you are a non -African American, you may or may not be exhibiting a symptom. If you live in America and have never discussed "race" in your family setting, you should suspect something is a little odd especially if you watch T.V.

Members of African American families that are reading the aforementioned and thinking, "what kind of family has not talked about "race" in America? He must be pulling my leg," should think about it for a minute. Yes, most families in America have talked about "race". However, many non African American, American families seldom come in contact with African Americans, and therefore have less reason to bring up the subject as a family discussion. Our observations indicate, that many culturally poisoned families don't bring it up because it puts painful, and unresolved, psychological baggage out in the open. Therefore, they simply ignore the subject when ever possible. In some African American families, we hear the phrase "don't start that Black talk again". That is a CP symptom.

The families most likely not to talk about "race" are mixed families that are culturally illiterate about each other's culture, or are culturally poisoned. This is because the "race" issue is a sensitive, and volatile subject between strangers, and this is doubly the case with mixed parents and partners. Race issues would bring up psychological issues that the parties would not be prepared to deal with, and could cause disharmony within the family, so the subject is therefore simply avoided. This is not unlike what we see in other areas where ethnic groups are in close contact such as the work place in America. Serious discussions on "race" are considered too politically dangerous and therefore avoided.

So in self-assessment the words you use or don't use for the people around you, can also give you a hint about your self-image.

The CP Snap shot: in questions one, and two we looked at how CP can effect your view of the world. In questions three, and four we looked at how CP can effect your view of various ethnic groups and History. In questions five and six we looked at how CP can effect the models we use for earthly, and spiritual behavior. In this last set of questions we are looking at how CP effects your self and group image. In question seven, we introduced the concept of Image AIDS. And raised the Bigger Question of Image Poisoning.

8. 50% Divorce Rate

Is the divorce rate 50% or higher all over the world? NO

It is common knowledge that **the divorce rate in America is on the rise**[xxxviii], so evidently the relationships between men, and women are on the decline. **But is this the case all over the world? No.** This is specifically a problem in western culture. Muslims, Jews and others don't suffer from this problem. As a part of American culture, we as African Americans are also suffering in our relationships with the opposite sex.

In Africa the divorce rate averages 8% in the cities despite significant western influence. In the rural areas (less western influence) it drops to 2%.[xxxix] **What are they doing that we are not?** They have Rites of Passage, which include relationship training. They are taught the expectations, and responsibilities of men, and women in a relationship. The training is evidently effective as demonstrated by the **98% relationship success rate in that culture.** Unfortunately, in western culture the training is by example only. Obviously, most parents are setting the wrong example. If you don't get relationship training from your parents, church or ethnic culture, you are then left to the T.V. or your friends. With that in mind, there is no wonder about the high divorce rate. Most **Americans manage their relationships by** what I call the **OJT** process (on the job training). The results speak for themselves.

If you and I were going to start a business, we would typically do a survey of the **best practices** in the particular market we were about to enter. If we **compared companies,** and one had a **98% success rate,** and the other had an **80% failure rate,** we would not need a business degree to determine which business model we should follow. The same holds true for starting a lifelong commitment, or marriage. One would try to emulate what the successful people were doing. So one can safely conclude that we

Westerners are in need of Rites of Passage to improve our probability for successful family structures—**family values that work.**

The impression we have received, that there is a **family crisis everywhere is false.** That is propaganda, which **clouds the issue.** And we don't want to go back to the American family values of the past. Those family values were immoral; they included, and often depended on enslaving other human beings. As mentioned earlier why would a Black person want to adapt those kinds of values? **Cultural Poisoning clouds the view of our mother country, Africa,** as a source of relationship information.

I must point out that one **gets out of something what one puts into it.** With that old adage in mind, look around for a standard American relationship school. There are no American Rites of Passage; Personal relationship training, or marriage training is not typically given in high schools or colleges. In fact when we look, what we find is marriage counseling centers. Those are usually places to go when your marriage is falling apart.

In America **we put little or nothing into relationship training,** and therefore we get little out. The comprehensive cultural training of the elder societies on the planet have been reduced to simple ceremonies, like the debutante ball where young ladies get dressed up and presented to "proper society" and are then left to fend for themselves.

An incorrect answer to the divorce question is an indication of **Ethnic Group AIDS.** That is an information deficiency regarding other ethnic groups. This information deficiency blinds Americans to the full range of relationship models that are available to them. In African Americans it is more specifically referred to as African Group AIDS.

African Group AIDS causes Group image poisoning, and a kind of cultural blindness that makes African Americans abandon our traditional relationship values, and adapt the first relationship model we see. In this case, the western relationship models we have had have not served us well. For adults changing these deep-seated western values we have learned may be very difficult, if not impossible. However, there is an opportunity for our youth, through cultural literacy, to expand their options, and generate better relationship statistics than their American parents have.

*　　　　　*　　　　　*

The Bigger Question: Group Image Poisoning and Ethnic Unity.

The Image you have of **your group is connected to your self-image** and visa-versa. The image you have of yourself, is connected to the image you have of your group. The divorce question is a group image question, which leads to the bigger questions related to the American group, and your ethnic group.

You will recall in the cultural literacy project overview, we pointed out that **culture is the glue** that holds a group of people together. Group AIDS is the disorder that weakens, or can destroy this glue. A lack of cultural glue makes any ethnic group less effective, not just in relationships, but in all other group endeavors. What is your image of your ethnic group? Is the image you hold of your group positive, neutral or negative, with respect to group unity and effectiveness?

The family is the basic human group in any society. It is the fundamental building block of any social group be it ethnic, or national. We already know that here in America we need to do a better job in this area. Improved relationship effectiveness is fundamental to forming functional families, and an effective Team America.

*　　　　　*　　　　　*

Here are two last questions related to team America. **Can we reduce cultural poisoning enough to enable us to make use of successful relationship models that exist with our International neighbors? Said another way; can we use high success rate information to solve** some of our **present problems**, which would better prepare us to be more effective in the future? I think we can.

They say ignorance is bliss. Well unfortunately, Cultural AIDS makes most Americans, to arrogant and falsely proud to absorb input form other ethnic groups regarding relationships, even when it is clear that others have been more effective in this area.

So the challenge of the Bigger Relationship Question is. Can our youth reduce Cultural Poisoning sufficiently to improve family unity, on the one hand and African American group unity on the other?

The CP Snap shot: in questions **one, and two,** we looked at how CP can effect your view of the world. In questions **three, and four** we looked at how CP can effect how you view various ethnic groups, and history. In questions **five, and six** we looked at how CP can effect the models we use for earthly, and spiritual behavior. In questions **seven, and eight** we are looking at how CP effects your self and group image. In question eight, we introduced the concept of group AIDS and African group AIDS. Then looked at the bigger question of Group image poisoning, and ethnic unity.

In the **ninth question,** on skin cancer we will be discussing the information deficiency, that is the **underlying cause for most of the other forms of AIDS.**

9. Skin Cancer Risk

Is everyone at high risk of getting skin cancer from staying in the sun? No

No, everyone is not at high risk of getting cancer from the sun. The sun is natural and necessary to life for most living things. **Some people are more susceptible than others** because of their biological make-up. The biology of human beings **differs** from person to person, and **from one ethnic group to another.** The biological reasons are well known, and a **wealth of information** has been compiled by a small segment of the medical community over the last 100 years.

If you answered yes to this question **don't feel like you are alone** on this one. This was one of the most astounding parts of my research. **90% of African Americans I interviewed answered this question YES.** This shows the lack of knowledge about what connects us to our African ethnicity, or how that Blackness functions to protect us. European Americans, and medical professionals responded similarly. These results indicate that neither **African Americans, nor** European Americans **know much about** the biological realities of **why we are different from one another.** The Kamitans (Egyptians) taught that the highest form of knowledge was self -knowledge. On the walls of their temples, and universities 6000 years ago they placed the words **"Man Know Thy Self".**

As their descendent 6000 years later in the spirit of that great challenge, I am proud to -present to you the following information. **Hopefully our children,** who may take this test, or some similar test in the next millenium, **will do better than we did** in respect to knowing themselves.

The scientific name for Blackness in the human body and in nature **is Melanin.** Melanin is the bio-chemical element in humans that **makes their skin dark.** Humans with **sufficient quantities of melanin** in their skin are **not at "high risk"** of getting cancer from the sun. Humans with insufficient melanin protection are at high risk of getting cancer from the sun.

This information should be common knowledge in the general medical community, and among the general public. It is not. In fact, for the most part it has been kept a secret. I refer to the secret as the Melanin Secret.

We will discuss four areas of information related to the sun/cancer question. (1) Biological differences in humans and the [A] empirical evidence, and [B] scientific evidence that support these facts. (2) We will discuss melanin and how it protects melaninated humans. (3) Cultural poisoning as it relates to melanin. We will also look at the bigger question of "race" (4) the "Race" Myth.

(1) Biological differences in humans

[A] Empirical Evidence

Melanin information has been written about by experts for experts and is very technical. However, recently African American researchers like Carol Barnes have tried to put this information in a form that the average person could understand. I have repackaged a small portion of this new user-friendly biological information, to provide you with a one-minute overview of the issue. You should understand that Africans are children of the sun. That is we are designed for efficient functioning in hot climates.

The biological basis of our blackness is melanin, as was mentioned earlier. It is the natural substance in our bodies that gives our skin pigment. We first appeared, and evolved on this planet in tropical sunny environments. Our bodies are designed to take maximum advantage of the benefits of the sun. Individuals with sufficient amounts of melanin in their bodies do not need sun block to stay in the sun.

Caucasian people are people of the ice. That is, their bodies are biologically adapted to functioning well in cold regions of the world. Who does overexposure to the sun pose a danger to? You don't need a doctor to give you the answer. We have all been to the beach with our European American friends, or colleagues and seen them get **sunburned to the point of their skin peeling off**. We have all observed that the sun affects different white people differently. Some are effected in a couple of hours; others fall asleep and get burnt. Still others get very red, and some just get a tan. Their limited supply of melanin gets energized from the sun, and their skin gets darker. We have all seen **former President Reagan going to the hospital to get skin cancer treatment** as a result, of too much exposure to the sun.

The sun is a danger to European people. Doctors warn de-melaninated individuals to look out for brown spots on their skin, for it could indicate skin cancer. Mr. Browder points out that the **American Cancer Society** ran adds **targeting White people** which warned them, that *any* **exposure to the sun could cause skin cancer**. Their message regarding unprotected sunbathing, was clear and to the point: *"If you fry now, you will pay later!"*

African Americans do not all have a full measure of protection from the sun either. I have heard **light skinned African Americans say that they too get sunburned**. This may be true. However, **let us not confuse the issue**. When I refer to Black people in the context of melanin and skin cancer, **I am referring to individuals with traditional** (native) **African skin pigmentation**. I.e. Brown to Blue Black. In that context, I have never heard of a strongly melaninated Black person being burned by the sun. Personally, I have never had sunburn, or anything that remotely feels like sunburn, and I have been out in the sun everyday all day for days at a time, in places like Hawaii. I wore nothing but my bathing trunks, and have never used sun block in my life. None of my doctors have ever told me to look out for brown spots on my brown skin.

Do you know or have you ever heard of a Black person with skin cancer, or of a Black person dying from skin cancer? **I haven't.** However, I am not a doctor or a medical researcher so I don't claim my observations are not open to challenge. If you have information to the contrary please write me and let me know, so that I will be better informed.

In conclusion, from empirical evidence you should have been able to answer the question correctly from what you already know. That is, **melaninated human beings have built in protection from the sun. Those without are naturally unprotected.** This information is actually part of your **common knowledge without the necessity of resorting to scientific data.** Now lets move on to the scientific data that reinforces the empirical evidence.

[B] Scientific Evidence

Why are Black people less likely to get skin cancer than White people?

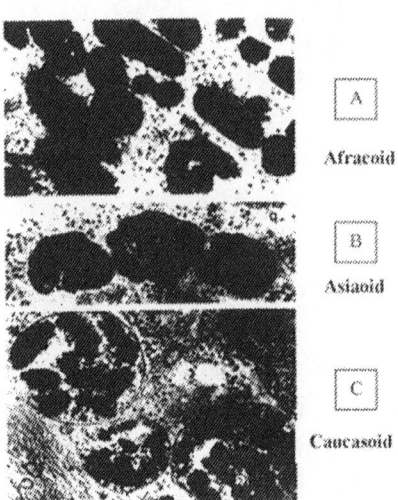

Figure 18 Melanin in three ethnic Groups

Because **Black skin is 100% more efficient** at screening out the harmful ultraviolet rays of the Sun. Ironically, those Caucasian men who have been in charge of the world's chemical production, have foolishly failed to live in accordance with nature, and thus have allowed chemicals to damage the ozone. The damage is referred to as the infamous **"hole in the ozone".** This man—made damage to the ozone is allowing more harmful radiation to reach the planet.

The scientist who discovered this phenomenon explained that the **ozone is responsible for filtering out the harmful solar ultraviolet radiation (UV rays).** UV rays are particularly dangerous to individuals who lack sufficient melanin protection.

It is **this combination of the lack of melanin and the loss of ozone UV protection** that has led to the warnings from the medical community, and the increase **in sun/skin related illnesses.** The increase in skin related illness effecting demelinated people include cancer, and herpes, which primarily effects Europeans.

Figure 18 shows the differences in melanin production in the three major ethnic groups: African, **Asian and Caucasian. A.** The **Afracoid** picture shows most of the melanosomes are individuated and the largest of the three groups. **B.** The **Asiaoid** malansome complexes are not as individuated, and contain some ground substance between the melanosomes. **C.** The **Caucasoid** complex is confined by a membrane and, contains a lot of small particles in addition to the relatively small malformed melanosomes.

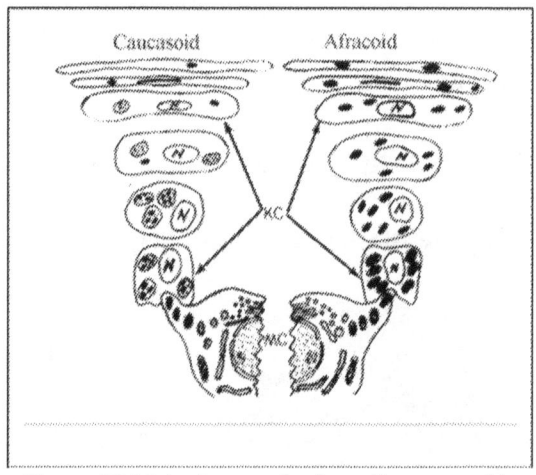

Figure 19 Melanin transfer from factory to skin

Figure 19 shows a **comparison between melanin preparation in Caucasian and African people.** This drawing illustrates the difference in size and density between the Afracoid and Caucasoid.

It is this **difference in melanin quality** that enables melanin to be more efficient in Black humans.

The [MC] melanocyte (melanin factory) transfers the melanosomes into adjacent (KC) keratinocytes (Skin Cells). You will note the fully formed melanosomes in the black person, and the broken up formation in Whites.

Mr. Carol Barnes, polymer chemist, lecturer, and noted melanin authority (and author of *Melanin* and *Jazzy Melanin*.) has delineated **six skin types,** noting their **relative susceptibility to skin cancer.** I have outlined the six types with some modifications below.

Type 1—these individuals are **White** and **cannot produce MELANIN.** They have blue eyes, blond or red hair, white skin and often have freckles. They have a Celtic background (Irish, Scottish, and Welsh).

They are **most prone** to develop melanoma, and other types of skin and organ cancer. Skin aging 25-30

Type 2—these individuals are **White** and **produce very low levels of MELANIN.** They have hazel or blue eyes. They have red or blond hair. They often have freckled skin.

They are **very prone** to developing skin cancer. (Non Celtic Caucasians) skin aging early 25-30 years old

Type 3—These individuals are **White** and produce **moderate to low levels of Melanin.** They have blond, brunette or lightly pigmented hair.

They show a **moderate to high risk** of developing skin cancer. Skin Aging 30-40

Type 4—These individuals are "**White**" *to* lightly tan and produce **moderate levels of MELANIN** They are lightly tan and include Japanese, Chinese, Greeks, Latino's, and Native Americans.

They show a **moderate risk** of developing **skin, or other organ cancer.**

Type 5—These individuals are **brown skinned.** They produce **moderate to high levels of MELANIN.**
Their eyes and hair are deep brown or black.
They include African Americans, Mexicans, Indians, Malaysians, Puerto Ricans, and other Latino's.
They **seldom develop skin cancers.** Skin aging after 50.

Type 6—These individuals are **Black in color** and can produce maximum amounts of Melanin.
Their eyes are dark brown or black, and their hair is BLACK.

They include **TRADITIONAL AFRICANS** (EGYPTIANS, ETHIOPIANS, NIGERIANS, ETC.), AFRICAN AMERICANS and AFRICAN AUSTRALIANS (ABORIGINES), Indians from S. India, etc.

They **virtually have no incidents of skin cancer!** Skin aging after 50-60 years old.

Note: I have reconstructed Mr. Barnes' chart pretty much as he has laid it out in his book[xl] (with his permission). With regard to the ethnic groups in each category, we should assume that there are exceptions. That is every individual in a particular ethnic group is not going to fit into a particular category. For example, the Puerto Rican ethnic group contains African, Puerto Ricans, and Caucasian, Puerto Ricans. They are obviously not all type 5's. Some members of the group may be type ones or sixes. Obviously you need to use common sense. The chart is a general guide (not a law) and there are exceptions.

Mr. Barnes' chart **does not explicitly mention two types of people:** Albinos and mixed[xli] blacks who are typically referred to as "light skinned" in the African American community. Albinos are individuals who through an accident of nature have virtually no skin pigment, and have light eyes, and light or white hair. Not being an expert in this area I would place the **albino in the Type 1** category based on the descriptions. Most **mixed individuals would fit in the type 4 and 5 categories** depending on their degree of de-melanization.

One additional **note on albinism:** I thought at one point that maybe there should be a separate category for Albinos as a special case. Upon reflection, **'Whiteness" is a mild form of Albinism.** That is, they are both highly susceptible to ill effects form intense exposure to the sun, and therefore should be in the same category as it relates to our discussion.

*　　　　　*　　　　　*

For instance, no one would recommend that either ethnic group make their home in equatorial Africa for fear of their life, and that of their children. Dr. King (1990) makes this point in a slightly different way by citing the following. **Most Albino, Cuna Indians living at the equator develop skin cancer by the age of seven** (Mc Fadden, 1961). Most White children living in New Guinea highlands on the equator also develop skin cancer before puberty (Daniels, 1972).[xlii]

(2) Melanin Protection as Measured by Science

The last chart shows the maximum dose of UV radiation (ultra violate rays) necessary **to cause degeneration in various skin types.** The chart makes graphically clear that a Type 1 White person requires far less exposure to the sun before his skin is negatively impacted then a Type 6 Black person.

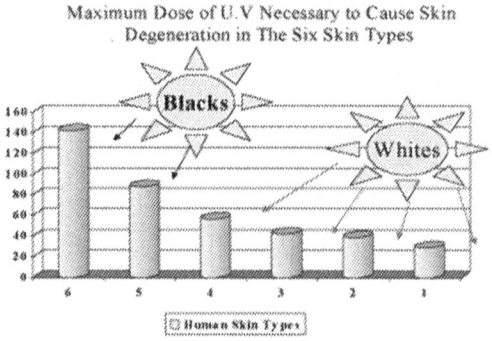

Table 1 U.V. Chart

The purpose of showing you this chart is to make it perfectly clear that modern science knows exactly how much protection the various ethnic groups have based on skin type. That is, they know as a matter of scientific fact that everyone is not at equal risk to the potentially harmful effects of the sun. Mr. Barnes has many other charts in his book. For instance, one illustrates the free radical production in skin. Quote: " Lack of melanin reduces one's ability to neutralize free radicals thus reducing an individual's resistance to skin cancer…."The point is scientists know a lot about melanin that has not been divulged to the American public.

Melanin knowledge (some people have more natural protection than others) is the basis for the production of **artificial sun protection products.** We generally call these products sun blocks. They can be found as stand alone products, or incorporated into products like skin tan lotion.

Every one can buy sun block at their local drug store without a prescription. The **rating system for sun block** as explained to me by a pharmacist goes like this: **SPF Rating** = Sun Protection Factor. SPF ratings range from a minimum of **15** to a Maximum of **45**. SPF 15 provides 92% coverage and SPF 30 provides 97% coverage. Ratings higher than 30 do not provide higher coverage. **My pharmacist could not correlate any of these standard ratings to skin types,** or even tell me if there was supposed to be a correlation. My pharmacist, who is "trained" on how to dispense this product from his drug store, might have been the wrong person to ask which sun block one should use. If you have more information about SPF ratings that would allow me to correlate them to skin types, please let me know.

The reason I dragged you through the technical SPF stuff is to point out that there appears to be a gigantic gap between **what science knows about melanin**, and what the average medical practitioner responsible for our health care knows about melanin. Doesn't it seem reasonable, given the scientific knowledge, which exists, that a person buying sun block, should be able to find a chart that explains how much artificial sun protection one should buy based on the amount of natural protection an individual already has? Or at least one should be able to expect that a trained medical "professional" could explain the information in the absence of such a chart. There is a reason why these common sense tools are not available.

Why is there this difference in scientific melanin knowledge, and medical practitioner's melanin knowledge? Is it simply to sell more of the higher SPF rated products, or is there more to it than that? I would suggest to you that it is more than that. For example, in all my years in American schools I have often heard the word Black used in both a positive, and negative sense. However, I have never heard the word "melanin" in any sense. Money or greed did not motivate this reality. American educational institutions purposely create melanin AIDS by the sin of omission. Melanin AIDS is a major factor in keeping cultural poisoning alive in America. Many myths have been constructed to keep melanin AIDS alive in the bio-computers of man.

(3) The Poison Sun Myth as it relates to melanin

The Poison Sun Myth is pervasive and shows up on T.V. more than any place else. The **T.V. commercials** for sun block lotion that **imply that we are all at high risk of getting cancer** from the sun, and therefore, we should run out and by their product **are misleading** at best. At worst these commercials further confuse people regarding their biological assets, and liabilities, and **facilitate cultural poisoning**. Whites and Blacks are not exactly equal. The reality is that we are biologically different. The fact that some human beings need to use **sun block SPF35** to protect them from the sun, **is just a demonstration of the reality of our differences**. Using the sun/dis-ease model to demonstrate one of the real differences between ethnic groups was done for a reason beyond explaining how to buy sun block.

Using the sun to demonstrate our differences is based on a simple idea. If the American "race" problems are based on our perceptions, or misperceptions of ethnic differences then it stands to reason that a better understanding of our actual differences should help reduce the problem. Whether the fears are a result of xenophobia (general fear of things differ-ent) or racism, knowledge can overcome them. The key to understanding ethnic difference, is knowledge of the biological melanin realities underly-ing those differences.

Melaninated skin has been the **biggest asset and the biggest liability** of people of color in America. As a liability it makes social integration easier to block by anti-humanists. Italian and Irish immigrants are often used as an example of well executed American assimilation. Whites have often said, "why don't Blacks stop complaining and just fit in like the other immigrants"?

First, African Americans are not immigrants. More importantly, people of color, unlike European immigrants are easy visible targets for anti-humanists. Incase you had not noticed melaninated skin is not an effective stealth weapon in a majority White society like America.

People's ignorance of our biological differences has enabled anti-humanists to utilize the **divide and conquer strategy** against humanists. Anti-humanist, have on the one hand misrepresented the real differences, and invented negative differences that don't in fact exist. These inventions are known as stereotypes. Stereotypes (obviously ridiculous generalizations about ethnic groups) have been very effective at keeping the humanists eyes of the prize. That is, if I can keep you busy chasing your tail trying to fix stereotypes, you will never even think of the concept of melanin AIDS, will you?

To kill off stereotypes, melanin must be **converted from its artificial liability** status back to its **original asset status.**

As we conclude, melanin is an asset and protection from the sun is only one of its values. It is found in its greatest quantity in the skin, and its greatest density in the genitalia. It is found in many other body centers. The road to Black /White harmony is paved with melanin. That is rather than allowing a few people to play on our ignorance about melanin, humanists need to better understand the reality behind ethnic biological difference.

*   *   *

The bigger Question: Why is there a big Melanin Secret?

The **bigger question** is why, since the experts know this information, has the reality of our differences been kept from medical professionals, and the public. **Who would benefit from not talking about melanin? What else don't you know about melanin that you should know?**

As mentioned earlier, **melanin has many other functions beyond basic sun protection.** Many African authors have indicated that Classical African Civilization had considerable functional melanin knowledge. However, modern science knows relatively little about the subject. It is only in the last 100 years or so that melanin science has come back into the scientific literature. As food for thought you will find a short list of where melanin can be found, and where you can see it at work. This will give you a feel for how melanin knowledge may be of value to you.

Table 2 Melanin locations and worktable

Melanin is found in major organs/other locations	Melanin is at work daily in these conditions
Heart	Memory/Memory retrieval
Liver	Intuition
Gastrointestinal tract	Motivation
Arteries	Movement (motor Output)
Skin (Our largest organ)	Sensory/Input
Eyes	Feeling sensations
Auditory nerves of the inner ear	Emotions
Testes, Epididymis (inside the testes)	Utilizing external energy sources (light, sound)
Brain—Neuromelanin	Anti-cancer
Ovaries	High spirituality ("shouting", "speaking in tongues"
interior of most cells of melaninated humans	Dreaming
Rivers, plants, , soil, and in space	Meditation and Trance

Naturally this is **only a partial list.** Let me make a final, and very important comment regarding melanin. There are harmful drugs that bind to, and alter the chemical reactivity of melanin. Mr. Barnes lists many of these drugs. The following are three you will recognize; cocaine, marijuana, and nicotine. This information raises many questions regarding African Americans' and addiction as well as the American drug scene in general.

Dr. Cress Welsing, in her famous book *The Isis Papers,* gives us the world's first psychological model for racism, and its variations. This model is called The Cress Theory of Color-Confrontation and Racism (White Supremacy): a Psychogenetic Theory and World Outlook—1970

The Cultural poisoning model, and the cultural literacy strategy is mainly concerned with the surface operational aspects of the psychological disorder we call cultural poisoning. Dr. Welsing's work is focused on the underlying causes, and motivational forces associated with color confrontation. Color confrontation is one of the dynamics of cultural poisoning. In short the "Cress theory" asserts that feelings of color inadequacy (lack of melanin), and fear of genetic annihilation is the underlying psychological disorder that results in excessively aggressive behavior by non-melaninated people. This last item of food for thought is complex, and you really need to get Dr. Welsing's book to get a feel for the full range of thought, and ramifications of her model. All Americans should read this book especially psychiatrists. African Americans should consider her work mandatory reading.

CP Test Snap Shot: we have looked at how cultural poisoning has affected Americans in many areas including our view of the world, of ethnic groups, how we see hero's and our spiritual views. In the last two questions, we looked at how CP impacts an individual's self and group image. Questions one through eight can be thought of as the "what" of cultural poisoning. That is to say, what areas of human endeavor does CP actually affect? The question we are presently completing discusses the underling "Why" behind cultural poisoning. That is, melanin AIDS is underneath all aspects of cultural poisoning as it pertains to the color issue.

The last question is focused on your family doctor, and deals with one of the behavioral results of cultural poisoning.

10. Family Doctor Choice

Does it make any difference what color your family doctor is? YES

Yes, it does make a difference what color your doctor is. **There is ethnic added value that a Black doctor brings** to the medical table for African Americans. It is not the case that doctors of another ethnicity cannot bring such value; it is just less likely.

Specifically, There are **four reasons why it does make a difference what color your doctor is.** The first, is the real **biological difference** in human beings, second is **economics**, third is **health safety,** and the fourth reason is **unique ethnic group needs**. The additional information we will discuss as a part of this answer is intended to cause you to think more critically about your health care. When you think about it, it will make sense that as you **evaluate your doctor's prices** and bedside manner, you should **also evaluate the ethnic factors** as well.

Unfortunately, due to space limitations this subject can get only the briefest treatment here.

Blacks are different. Sickle cell anemia is one example. Your Black doctor is more likely to be medically knowledgeable about these differences out of self-interest if nothing else.

Economics: You should go to a Black doctor for the same reason you should go to a black lawyer, dentist, or retail store. It makes good economic sense to spend your money in your ethnic community.

Health and Safety: A person who suffers from the mental disorder of racism does not become cured when he, or she puts on his doctor's uniform, or his police uniform. I do not want to make you paranoid about going to the doctor. However, we have all heard stories about what doctors have done to patients without their knowledge, so a certain amount of common sense caution is in order.

Ethnic group needs: Just as an Asian may go to an Asian doctor who understands yin and yang there is cultural comfort, and a medical value added that going to a culturally literate African doctor can provide. An example, would be a great Afrikan American female doctor in New York Dr. Justice who is culturally literate and well steeped in the Afrikan tradition. She is often on the radio in New York. If you ever have an opportunity to listen to her, you will immediately be aware that she is discussing medically related cultural issues, that most European American doctors would be unaware of, let alone prepared to discuss with their Patients.

*   *   *

The Bigger Question: The Ethno-neutral medicine Myth and dysfunctional ethnic group behavior

The Western medical establishment asserts that all **medicine** should be **practiced without regard to ethnicity.** To a certain degree, I feel that is morally correct and a practical necessity so I agree with that assertion as far as it goes. However, to ignore that there is a biological difference in humans is at best fool hardy and at worst criminal. I assert that in addition to ethno-neutral medicine, "**ethno-centric medicine**" should be practiced whenever necessary. Doing otherwise is to deny and defy reality.

The four reasons I give in support of the main question are **also the supporting arguments for the bigger question:** killing off the culturally poisoned notion of ethno-neutral medicine. In light of the recent move by the medical community toward "holistic" medical approaches, purposely leaving out ethnicity from the wholeness of medical practice is an anti-humanist if not racist act.

American **doctors** as a general rule are **not taught about melanin** in medical school. So how can they provide complete comprehensive medical care to people who are strongly melaninated? If Doctors do not have all the information they should have about melaninated patients, then non-melaninated patients suffer as well. Everyone wants to have access to the most completely trained doctors possible.

Now don't get me wrong, **if you are in a car accident go to the nearest hospital**. But when you plan your care, you have a choice. Think about it.

*　　　　　*　　　　　*

The bigger question part II is African American economic literacy.

Is your economic behavior positive, neutral, or negative regarding the economic well being of your group? As a group African Americans behave as if they are economically illiterate. If you spend your money out side of your own community, You should not wonder why your community is poor as Malcolm said, "it is supposed to be poor. You sent all the money out". Don't you think its time for us to get rid of this "group" economically dysfunctional behavior, and become more economically effective?

We need for instance to once again take control of melanin science. In Classical Afrikan Civilization, Afrikans went to kametic doctors versed in melanin science. Black doctors who are getting paid are in a better position to contribute to, and participate in melanin science.

So for an African American to go to a Black doctor makes good economic sense.

Remember, the **answers** to these questions are **designed to make you think**! And in the case of economics you also need to act by putting your money where your mouth is.

CP Test Snap Shot: we have looked at how cultural poisoning has affected Americans in many areas including our view of the world, of ethnic groups, how we see hero's and our spiritual views. In the last two questions, we looked at how CP impacts an individual's self and group image.

Questions one through eight can be thought of as the "what" of cultural poisoning. That is to say, what areas of human endeavor does CP actually affect? Question nine introduced us to melanin AIDS. Question ten looked at the four reasons African Americans should use African American Doctors. Finally, we looked at the Bigger Ethno-neutral medicine and economic question.

CONGRADULATIONS you have completed the test, and the main part of the book. You started out by taking the test, and then uncovering the Cultural Literacy projects answers to each of the questions. In the next section, the Test Review you will get a look at the reasoning behind the test and instructions on how you can rate yourself.

TEST REVIEW (A PSYCHOGRAPHIC DESCRIPTION)

The test review will outline for you the **thinking and rationale behind the creation of the Self-Test**. The review will **also point out what the test is not**. We will then moves on to your personal bottom line where you will grade yourself based on your original answers (Thoughts) to the test. The last sentence wasn't a typo; it was just an ebonics test to see if you were paying attention.— ☺

First, let me get some test house keeping out of the way regarding what the test is, and what it is not. It is **not an. absolute measurement** of your degree of Cultural Poisoning. At best **it is a relative measurement** of your cultural orientations

Scientists measure things in absolute terms. For instance, they can measure the exact **speed of a car** with scientific instruments. They can tell you that a specific car is traveling a **100.567989 miles per hour.** They can also clearly correlate this speed with reality, that is relate this speed to an object on the earth that is standing still, or another moving object like a second car. Individuals who engage in racing automobiles utilize this type of scientific technology all the time. They use this type of measurement tool to determine how the adjustments they have made to the cars have affected the car's performance, and handling behavior. The self-test is not that kind of exacting technology. However, it is intended to help you fine-tune your mental performance, and personal behavior.

The Self-test is a **new piece of social science technology,** not a scientific tool like a ' speedometer. Human beings are obviously too complex for that kind of analysis given the current state of western psychological tools.

The Self-Test is an early yet timely pass at measuring relative cultural poisoning as we move into the next century.

The test attempts to measure different things in different people. Attempting to meet this objective has proved exceedingly difficult. As a result, you will note that **some questions are more geared towards one group than another.**

The premise of the test is simple. Of the three Major ethnic groups, **Europeans and Asians** when asked questions, or when they are talking about their ethnic group **respond positively. Africans** on the other hand exhibit a disproportionate level of **negative responses** regarding their group.

It is also the case that **European and Asian** Americans who are positive about their group are also significantly **less positive about the African group.**

The challenge then becomes, can some of the cultural poisoning which exists in all ethnic groups to varying degree's be identified, and or adjusted by a home based self-test? Said another way, people can now test themselves for pregnancy, and diabetes in the home and take appropriate action, why not **include cultural poisoning in the new self-help movement?**

To demonstrate what I mean **ask a European American about his group** and you will find that he, or she typically values and is proud of their heritage. He will typically tell you proudly that his European ancestors made great contributions to the history of mankind by bringing the wold medicine, Philosophy, Religion etc.

If you **ask an Asian American** you will generally get a similar response valuing and praising their ethnic group, and their ancestor's contributions; spiritual, medical, philosophical, etc.

Ask an African American the same question, and you fairly often will get a response that indicates that the respondent neither values, nor is proud of their culture.

It is not uncommon to hear an African American upon being addressed as such say, "I am not an African American I am an American. **I have**

nothing to do with Africans. I was born here." Or as a popular Dark skinned (heavily melaninated) African American radio talk show host said on National T.V. " I'm not Black and…. I'm never going to be Black…or associated with all those negative things…". It is interesting to note that these same individuals are perfectly comfortable using descriptive terms like European American, Asian American, or Native American but have a Brain Crash on the equally legitimate description African American. This form of reality denial is sometimes referred to as Head in the Sand Syndrome, or Whoopi Goldberg syndrome. It is interesting to watch this **anti-African argument presented by African Americans,** and it obviously raises some questions about the state of cultural health of such individuals.

The question upon **observing this phenomena** becomes, is the person responding with knowledge regarding their ethnic group's history/culture and then rejecting it as invaluable, or something unworthy of pride? Or is the individual simply culturally illiterate?

The Cultural Literacy Project is based on the premise that these individuals while often well "educated" in the western sense of the word (trained for a particular job or career) are culturally illiterate regarding the culture of their ancestors, and have no knowledge of Classical African Civilization. And that this particular form of **illiteracy can be corrected in most people,** just as reading skills can be improved in most illiterate individuals.

While European and Asian Americans can provide you with information regarding the contributions of their group both here in America and in their Mother land, few African Americans can do the same. This **lack of basic cultural information** is what I refer to as cultural illiteracy. Most Non-African Americans suffer from a similar level of illiteracy when it comes to information regarding the full scope, and value of African contributions to the forward movement of mankind.

The Self-Test makes the positive assertion that the missing information, and misinformation **can be detected and corrected** by the individuals themselves. So while Cultural Illiteracy is not the sole cause of cultural poisoning it is a **precondition for CP.**

The test is **designed to detect the presence of cultural AIDS** in the different ethnic groups in the following ways.

If you are African American the questions were designed to assist you in understanding for yourself whether your answers reflect a **predominance of Eurocentric or "Afrocentric" thought** orientation. Said another way; do you view yourself and the world through European glasses, Afrikan glasses, or some combination of the two? If your view is a combined view which part of the combination is dominant?

There is a need to address one criticism that comes up from the African American community. That is **"this is a test of how black you are."** While this is sometimes said in the proper context more often than not it is a misinterpretation of the test's objectives. Understand that there are two **types of Blackness, Biological and Psychological.** Biological blackness can be more or less detected by looking in the mirror. If your eyes are not functioning ask any White person in America and they will tell you the answer. The test is aimed at helping you identify for yourself, your psychological orientation to Blackness in general, and your cultural orientation to yourself and your ethnic group.

If you are a European American what is your orientation to blackness in particular and people of color in general? The test is intended to assist you in determining for yourself if you are a part of the problem or part of the solution. You are being asked to think about your role in building Team America. Are you culturally poisoned? Is cultural poisoning reducing your effectiveness or hampering your interaction with other ethnic groups?

If your are Asian or of mixed ethnicity you will recall that a lack of ethnic understanding (cultural illiteracy regarding the historic behavior of European Americans) resulted in Japanese Americans being, suddenly and with out warning, put into concentration camps in America by the tens of thousands. How well do you know yourself and those with whom you work and live? Could the trucks come for you again?

The bottom line behind the test review i.e. the disclaimers and the structure of the test is to make clear to you that the objective of the test is not really to produce the score that you will create for yourself in the next section. It is to **cause you to think** more deeply than you may have, in the past; about who you are, who you want to be, and who you ought to be. It is to cause you to think about what you can do within yourself to improve your ethnic, and interethnic performance and behavior. Unlike a racecar, a team of people will not be responsible for changing your cultural poisoning (or it's effects upon you). **You must in fact change yourself.**

The last part of the test review is intended to tell you a little about the structure of the test. Each of the questions was chosen for a specific reason, and fits into three categories of detection/ correction. (1) Geographic Cultural Orientation (2) Personal and Group philosophy and (3) Western Worldview Orientation.

*   *   *

THE QUESTION MAP

Geographic Cultural Orientation
1. Map distortion question   Geographic AIDS
2. The continent question   Worldview AIDS
3. Classical African Civilization   Historic AIDS
question

Personal and Group philosophy
7. The good hair question   Image AIDS
9. Skin Cancer question   Melanin AIDS
3. Classical African Civilization   Historic AIDS
question
10. Your Doctors Ethnicity   Medical AIDS and
question   Economic AIDS

Western Worldview Orientation

4. Columbus "discovery" question	American AIDS
5. George Washington hero Question	Hero AIDS
8. World wide 50% divorce rate question	Ethnic Group AIDS

Besides noting that **question three has relevance in two categories** space restricts my comments.

Now **lets move on to your personal bottom line.** With the understanding that the next section is not an exercise wherein I, the author tell you where you are with your ideas. Rather it is **an exercise of you telling yourself where you are** with respect to the information presented in our discussion.

YOUR PERSONAL BOTTOM LINE

The questions in this test covered general public knowledge that most Americans would know something about, what you might refer to as **common knowledge**. That is information that you know, believe, or have an opinion about. Hopefully, one of the things that the test made clear is that common knowledge is not necessarily common. I hope reading the answers caused you to **Think!**

This is the **end of part one of your debriefing**. This is where you look at your original ideas (how you answered the questions), compare them with the information presented to you, and reach your own personal bottom line regarding your degree of cultural poisoning and what it means to you, your ethnic group and building Team America (creating harmony).

*   *   *

Let's **review the results** and discuss what they mean. Below the test has been reproduced with the answers. Grade yourself by checking the answers with your answers, and recording the results in the box marked grade.

1. Were all the **maps** we learned from in school more or less accurate? **NO**

2. How many **continents** are there? **6** is Europe one of them? **NO**

3. **In what country is Classical African Civilization** located? **Kamit (Egypt)**

4. Did **Columbus** discover America? **NO**

5. Does President **George Washington** represent a hero to all Americans? **NO**

6. Are the popular Western pictures of **Jesus Christ** consistent with his physical description in the Holy Bible? **NO**

7. Do you, a member of your family, or a friend of yours have **good hair**? **NO**
(That is, would you agree that straight or curly hair is more desirable then "kinky" hair)?

8. Is the **divorce rate** 50% or higher all over the world? **NO**

9. Is everyone at high risk of getting **skin cancer** from staying in the sun? **NO**

10. Does it make any difference what color your **family doctor** is? **YES**

Grade_____each question is worth 10 points all ten correct =100%
give your self half credit if you were partially correct.

*   *   *

Self Test Results
Cultural poising index

<u>% of questions correct</u>

100%   **Closet Poisoning**

75%   **Minor Poisoning**

50%   **Seriously poisoned**

25%   **Critically poisoned**

0%   **Acutely poisoned.**

CP Index Descriptions

It is impossible to grow up, be educated and live in America and **not
suffer from some degree of cultural poisoning.** We live in the west, and
what is taught in our schools is the good, and bad of the western worldview. The University level is usually the **first time you have the option of
African Studies or Asian studies.** Understand that there has **never been
any intent** on the part of the American educational system to teach the
African worldview, or the Asian worldview. You will note that to the
extent that these courses exist they are a **result of pressure from those particular ethnic groups.** Today, while Asian studies suffer less of an attack,

all ethnic studies are under attack and to an extent their **progress is in remission**. This remission is due to what has been called the "White backlash". That is the culturally poisoned notion those ethnic groups have made too much progress in America and should be slowed down.

The White Backlash is an example of the culturally poisoned negative reaction to progress in humanism. This is not healthy for America. Those proponents of the backlash, who took this test, will typically **fall into the last two categories of cultural poisoning**. Let's review the four cultural poisoning descriptions to better understand how this works.

Four Cultural Poisoning Categories

100% Closet Poisoning: means that this particular **test did not reveal any elements of cultural poisoning that you were not already aware of.** Hopefully, the bigger questions associated with each question provided you with additional information, and may have indicated area's of thought you might want to give consideration to. You are naturally to be commended for recognizing the most common area's of poisoning, and correcting the programs in your bio-computer. If you never had the poisoning programs, then your parents deserve the commendation.

75% Minor Poisoning: You or your parents are also to be commended if you scored in this category. This category indicates that your degree of **poisoning is relatively narrow**. For instance, you may have determined that you need to work on personal poisoning, and that group poisoning is not as big an issue for you or visa versa. You may only be infected by a couple of cultural viruses, Congratulations.

50% Seriously Poisoned: indicates you have a **typical amount of poisoning**. This amount of poisoning might be expected in the American educational and social environment. Your worldview education has been omitted, and in fact your education actively works to suppress, or otherwise prevent the integration of thought processes from other worldviews into your range of thinking.

0% Acutely Poisoned: indicates an **excessive amount of poisoning**. You are completely overcome by cultural poisoning. You need to realize that you are probably a **cultural danger** to your children, other members of your family and American society in general.

If your are **African American and fall into this category then** go out and slit your throat now for you are a **danger to your "race"** (only kidding). Hopefully, you are not Clarence Thomas but you could be in danger of becoming one. If you got 0% correct then **you have answered the questions like I would have 20 years ago**. You are facing a complex personal issue that must be resolved. However, if you have read this far in the book and are still with me then you're on the right track. We **look forward to standing shoulder to shoulder with you** in the fight against cultural poisoning. Good luck.

These categories also represent a **range of behavioral possibilities** that present a threat to other human beings. These range from **mild prejudice to a criminally insane** racist who is a physical danger (possibly a potential murderer) to other human beings. Examples include **killer cops** (who shoot children, grandmothers, etc)

If you are Caucasian American and rated in this category, then you should understand **that you are most likely an anti-humanist if not a cultural terrorist**. Or you could be a very badly poisoned Humanist. If you are a humanist it is important to understand that even though you may not be inclined to kill, or consciously harm, or deprive others of their human rights you can still suffer from high degrees of cultural poisoning. If you are **completely overcome by cultural poisoning**, this means that your only frame of reference is the western worldview. You need to broaden your perspective if you plan to positively participate in the multi-ethnic America you will be living in during the next century. If you are not a mortal enemy who is reading this book for alternative motives and you are still with me, then you too are on the right path. We also **look forward to standing shoulder to shoulder with you** in the fight against cultural poisoning.

No matter what color you are, no matter what degree of cultural poisoning you suffer from, **you have work to do.** The good news is that just as the **alcoholic who admits** he is a drunk has taken the **first step** to curing his/her illness, the **admission that cultural poisoning exists,** and that you suffer from it to some degree is a **first step.** A first step in becoming a more informed and more effective ethnic citizen, American citizen and humane world citizen.

When you think about your degree of cultural poisoning you should **think about what you have been taught** in the western educational system **versus what other world citizens have been taught.** Have you ever noticed that when you meet an Asian, or continental Afrikan they are always quite knowledgeable about the western world? That's because in Asia, and in Africa in addition to being taught their own worldviews they are also, as a matter, of course, taught the western worldview. The result is that the individuals from these cultures are **multi-worldviewists.** That is, they are familiar with **at least two worldviews,** and sometimes all three. This gives them an advantage in the new global competition.

They marvel at the **general cultural illiteracy of Americans.** A recent statistic that caught my eye was a study that indicated something like **80% of American high school students could not find Canada** on the map. If a student can't find his National neighbor on the map, it is certain that he would not for instance know where the land described in the bible is located, or where the 100 million Afrikans in Asia live. It is precisely this **cultural poisoning induced Worldview illiteracy** that enabled American leadership to **convince some of the American people** to allow an attack on a nation like Vietnam, which posed no threat to the United States. The United States badly underestimated the will of the Vietnamese people, due to a lack of understanding of their worldview. Worldview illiteracy is not a harmless state of affairs. In America it has unnecessarily cost us the loss of ten's of thousands of American lives. **What you don't know can more than hurt you it could literally kill you or your children.**

The American educational **system has to be redone,** in order to produce productive world citizens capable of making a positive contribution to the new—global village of the next century. Specifically people must be educated in cultural literacy, in the broad sense of the word. Our schools should adapt a complete worldview orientation that comprises all three worldviews. This way our children who are our future will be better prepared, and effectively armed with a New World View that will help promote the unity, and harmony in America, and in the world.

A world citizenship education would accomplish three things for future Americans (1) Enable our citizens to interact on the social, economic, and political level from an informed orientation of mutual respect, and understanding. (2) Enable American businesses to be more competitive in the new global economy. (3) Enable our nation to construct more humanistic, and realistic foreign polices that will lead world thought into the next millenium, and make positive contributions to the global village of the future.

Finally, **my comments on the on going voucher question in America.** It is not a matter of either/ or. We need both. Yes, we must have our own community based, owned, and operated schools. These schools must be funded by any means necessary including our tax dollars, because no one can argue with the positive results that they have produced in our children thus far. We must also insist that our public schools produce a better quality product. That means well-educated children, who will go on to be world class, productive, and positive citizens! Realistically history teaches us that the public schools will not rise to the occasion without first being challenged. So if the vouchers pose such a challenge then I say "I'm all for them! It's all good." After all, whatever serves to get this educational ball rolling has to be good. And we definitely don't want to lose any more of our children as we already have been. So let's not waste any more time arguing about this subject, our children can't wait.

*　　　　　　*　　　　　　*

Before we conclude let me leave you with one last question.

Are African Americans full and complete citizens of America to exactly the same legal degree as all other American citizens?

The **answer is no.** We are the only group of **"Renewable citizens in America"**. That's right, Americans must renew African American citizenship every twenty-five years. The next renewal is in 2007. Yes, in the year 2007 thirty-eight states must agree to renew African American "citizens'" right to vote. President Reagan was the last president to sign off on the temporary voting rights law extending it for another 25 years.

Think about it! Most Americans understand that African Americans may not be equal politically, economically, and socially with the majority population in America. But they honestly believe the legal battle has been completely won. They think African Americans are citizens with the **same permanent rights of all citizens in America.**

Unfortunately this idea of African American citizenship is **not consistent with reality.** The great American Attorney Dr. Robert Brock has carried the fight for permanent full enfranchisement of African American citizens, through all the courts of the land to the Supreme Court of the United States. The United States government has acknowledged the legal issue, but has not seen fit to resolve it.

Think About it; how is it that everyone in the world with access to TV knows about the O.J. Simpson trial, and almost no one knows about the **Leonard Ashton and 49 million African Americans vs. the United States of America.** African Americans vs. the U.S. is probably the most important case that was ever brought before the Supreme Court of this land, yet there is not a word on the news, or in our schools about this case.

*　　　　*　　　　*

Part I Summary

At the end of PART I CULTURAL POISONING, We will start as we began with a series of questions.

Who is controlling the information you receive and why? What happens when people mix up truth with false hood? What else have you been lead to believe that is not consistent with reality, and how will it effect you and your children in the future?

In the pursuit of answers to this series of questions, we introduced you to the Cultural Literacy Project with it problem analysis, and Solution Strategy models. We went on the review the answers to the Cultural Poising Self-Test, and in the end you gave yourself your own bottom line CP rating.

To the extent that 90% of all Americans suffer from some degree of Cultural Poisoning, most readers reviewing the answers gained some new information. Our individual mark on the test says we have some work to do. That is we all need to continue to ask ourselves some questions and provide our own answers in a way that raises our Cultural Literacy, and continues to reduce our Cultural Poisoning.

Last we left you with an African American question that we should all know more about.

Are African Americans full and complete citizens of America, to exactly the same legal degree as all other American citizens?

This question is even more important given the events leading up to **9/11/01** and the immediate aftermath.

Many African Americans in Florida did not have their votes counted. Bush II's Brother heading up state government in FL. and our "justice" system assisted **King Bush II** in bushwhacking the Presidency. Bush speaking for America (along with Israel) disrespected the nations of the world, and people of color by leaving the United Nations World Conference Against Racism. Then the United States was attacked. Instead of a Global War on Racism we have a Global War on "Terrorism". Congress in the dead of night passed a "law" called the PATRIOT ACT. Now people can be picked up off the street at random, and put in jail for an indeterminate amount of time.

Up until now we have mostly been talking about some older DoubleSpeak words like "Negro". Using your ability to detect Cultural Poisoning words, and phrases, should be used on newly invented words of our time as well. What does "citizen" mean really when it is applied to an African American, Native American, Arab American etc? **Who is a "terrorist'** and who is a freedom fighter, and who is telling us who is who? The Patriot Act, now that is a hot one. Who could possibly be against a "patriot" act? Now if that does not sound like a Big Brother Creation right out of Orwell's 1984 nothing does. So my fellow Americans keep your antennas up these are dangerous times.

To continue learning about Cultural Poisoning and to meet like-minded Cultural Soldiers join us on-line.

There are **Cultural Literacy 101 Clubs** at Delphi.com (biggest), MSN, Yahoo and other locations in CyberSpace. From time to time I have Cultural Literacy 101 Live (Audio Chat / Internet Radio Show), Join us live on-line up close and personal, check our Web Site Cultural Literacy Central for details, time and place etc.

When you come to CyberSpace be prepared to answer the Cultural Literacy projects most popular Cyber Question; What Makes you Black?

Now that you have completed the Cultural Poisoning part of the book, lets move on to part II Cultural Literacy.

PART II

CULTURAL LITERACY

THREE CULTURAL LITERACY MINUTES

Now That you have completed Part I your introduction to Cultural Poisoning, we can move on to the second part of the book, and your introduction to some of the **basic elements of Cultural Literacy** (CL). To convey this information, I will be using what we call Cultural Literacy Minutes (CLMin). A CLMin is a compact burst of information utilizing visual or Audio Tech-tools to add information to your cultural database. A CLMin is not a full discussion of a subject. It is an introduction it puts info on your radar screen. You must do the work of getting the detail to fully raise your cultural literacy regarding a given subject.

The Three CL Minutes we will cover are The Racespeak Model, African Aunk, and The Cultural War. The Race Speak Model gives you the bigger picture regarding cultural poisoning (CP). CP dose not just effect us here in America it effects world groups, and worldwide ethnic relationships. The African Aunk introduces you to the most widely know symbol in Classical African Civilization (CAC). The Cultural War introduces you to the war of Worldviews from the first attack on CAC to the present. The following is a brief introduction/description of each model:

The Racespeak Model

On the next page is a model we call the racespeak model. It is **in three parts**, the top, of the model is the racespeak engine. It is where positive and negative racespeak is generated. The middle, of the model is the **Ethnic Star Graphic.** It shows the three major ethnic groups, and their associated worldview databases. And at the bottom, is a **decision box,** which depicts three directions, America and the world can go in regarding how they deal with the "race" problem. The model can be used to take any word through the model and determine if it is a positive or negative race-speak word and why. The objective of the model is to assist individuals in determining, what is culturally poisoned language (corrupted language/reality) and why. For more info on this or any of the CLMin Email me or join a Cultural Literacy 101 Club in cyberspace.

The African Aunk

The CLMin on the Aunk is an introduction to the symbols, and thinking of the Classical Africans of Kamet. Anyone interested in Classical African Civilization, should have a working knowledge of African classical models. The models are the shortest routes to understanding the remarkable information the civilization has to offer. The Aunk originates in the Nubian/Kametian civilization, and is the oldest symbol/model of its type in recorded history. It is one of many such African symbol/models like the Pyramids, the Tree of Life, and the Magic Wand of Tehuti (Caduceus—Symbol we still see today in most American hospitals).

It is easily the most popular African symbol known to Africans here in America. Some Americans mistake it for a Christian cross. It is not a cross. The one page introduction to the Aunk gives you four examples of its use as a model. The four examples are just four of hundreds of concepts, the Aunk is capable of modeling. The Aunk, is a model that represents a form of cosmological thought requiring Afrikan 3D thinking skills. It was designed so that it would be a universal multi-disciplinary model, that would be capable of modeling both existing concepts, and concepts not yet in the human consciousness. The example of the Aunk as a model of the computer, is a demonstration of the Aunk's universality and timelessness.

The Cultural War

The CLMin on the War is a summary of what has come to be called the cultural war. Unfortunately, little or no definition has been put on this loosely kicked around term in America. There are actually two tables. One is a four stage high level view of the war, and the other is a more detailed history of the ten major battles of the war. As in any war, if the troops can not find the battlefield, it is obvious that they are headed towards disaster. The models start on the next page with the racespeak model.

The Racespeak Model

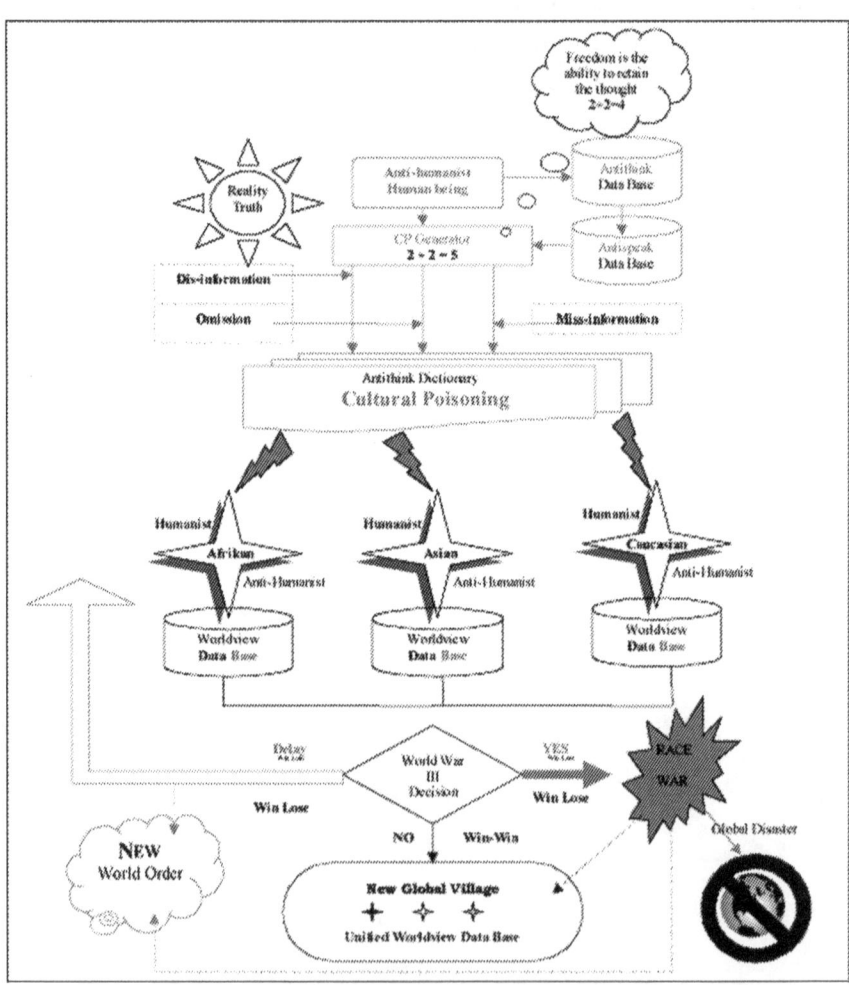

Figure 6 Racespeak engine, Ethnic star model and the Decision box

You will notice that the ethnic star model has humanists, and anti-humanists in each group. The other thing, you should keep in mind is that, the three major ethnic groups contain many sub-ethnic groups. For example, the Asian ethnic group contains the Japanese, Chinese the Tibetans and others. So which way will inter-ethnic relations lead us in the third millenium, to a New World Order, a Race War, or to the New Global Village? Now on to Classical Afrikan Civilization.

The African Aunk
More then 10,000 man years of thought

The Aunk (ankh) is known as the **Key to Life.** It is a symbol and some say a practical electronic device. But most importantly what makes it at key? It is a key because it is a model (Blueprint). The Aunk is one of many symbols/models that are essential to Afrikan Cultural Literacy.

The Aunk is a model of classical African concepts, and modern concepts. It is a universal way of looking at the world. Now lets look at the individual **physical parts** separated so you have a clear image of them in your mind's eye.

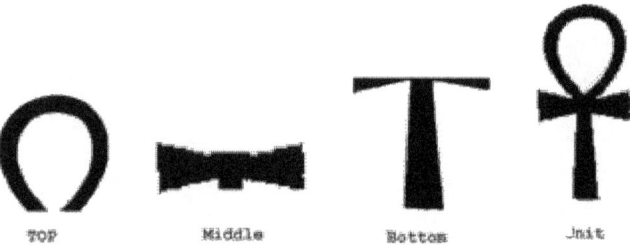

TOP   Middle   Bottom   Unit

Aunk as a model for classical concepts

Aunk as the fundamental principle in nature: Duality
    Top   female
    Middle   The parts have a relationship that unite them as one
    Bottom   male
    Unit: Duality Principle

1. Aunk Blueprint for reproducing life

Top	female vagina
Middle	male and female united in copulation
Bottom	male penis
Unit:	**Reproduction of life**

Element Theory
- **Complements**
- **Opposites**
Magnetism (+/-)   **Likes Attract**   **Opposites repel**

2. Aunk as model for thinking (true/false decision making)

Top	True (decided the thing or event is true)
Middle	Undecided (not enough facts, suspended judgement)
Bottom	False (decided the thing or event is false)
Unit:	**The decision making process**

3. Aunk as model for the human spirit

Top	Spirit
Middle	Mind
Bottom	Body
Unit:	**Human spirit**

The first symbol/model   **Anyone interested in**   **Classical African Civilization**   **Must learn**

Aunk as a model for the present

1. Aunk as model for computers

Top	Zero (0)
Middle	logical relationships (And, or, Nand, Nor)
Bottom	one (1)

Unit: Base 2 math model and computer logic model

The Cultural War

A high level view of the war

The cultural war, is a war of worldviews with 12 distinct battles. At the highest level, the war can be described simply by its four phases. See table 1 below

Table 3 The four Phases of the Cultural War

#	Phase	Attitude & Behavior	Location	Cultural Orientation	Dates
1	Afrikan	Afrikan and Proud	Africa	Culturally Literate	<1492
2	1st American	Ashamed to be African	America	Culturally Poisoned	>1492
3	2nd American	I'm Black and I'm proud	America	Reduced Poisoning	1960's
4	2nd Afrikan	Black proud and know why	America & Afrika	Cultural Literacy Returns	2000 +

One way to think of the cultural war is in terms of African attitude, and behavior in connection to the **four major dates**. Before Columbus (<1492), After Columbus, (most of the time we have spent in America), in the 1960's when African Americans start to recover from cultural poisoning. And finally 2000 forward, with renewed culturally literate attitudes and Behavior, African Americans moving into the new millenium.

Table 4 African Name History

#	Names	Source	Notes
1	Alkabu-laners	Afrika	Originated by Africans on the continent as per Dr. Ben
2	Kamitans	Afrika	Represents part of Afrika, Kamit (Egypt) meaning the Blacks
3	Ethiopians	Afrika (Greeks)	Represents part of Afrika, the land from Nubia/Kamit to India
4	Africans	Afrika (Romans)	Originated in Afrika used by the Romans and now everyone
5	**Negroes**	Europe (Whites)	Invented by Whites there are no such people
6	**Niggers**	Anti-Humanist	Invented by White racist to support their belief system
7	**Coloreds**	Europe (Whites)	Invented by Whites to describe Africans mixed with Whites
8	**Blacks**	Afrikans/AA	Physical description of melaninated people
9	African Americans	Africans	Denotes one of African and American lineage
10	Afrikans	Afrikans	Culturally literate Black people around the world

Notice the difference in the character of the names Afrikans called themselves when they and everyone else knew who they were, versus the names others called Afrikans when they knew nothing about their history on this planet. Look at the names we are now calling ourselves as we remember who we are.

Table 5 The Names war correlation

#	Names	Cult. War Phases
1	Alkabu-laners	
2	Kamitans	1
3	Ethiopians	
4	Africans	
5	Niggers	
6	**Coloreds**	2
7	Negroes	
8	**Blacks**	3
9	African Americans	
10	Afrikans	4

Table 3 makes the point that **history records a direct relationship** between what we call ourselves and our attitude and behavior. **Hip Hop youth** who use the "N" word as a name and call their woman "B's and Whores should take particular note of this correlation. As minister Farrakhan has pointed out if you figure out how to stop killing yourselves you may again figure out how to live to be 500 or 1000 years old.

History of the Cultural War

As you are already aware Human **history goes back some 3.5 million years**. Most of that history takes place on the African continent. When we move from prehistoric time to recorded history, we note approximately **10,000 years of Afrikan high culture** (civilization) recorded in the historical, and archeological records. We call this period the **Afrikan Classical period** of the Central worldview in the same way that the Greek period is known as the, classical period of the western worldview. Afrikan historians and scholars advise us that the first 8,500 years of recorded history, is dominated by the Afrikan worldview as there was no other "civilization" yet entered in recorded history. You should note that African scholars measure recorded history from the time of the Kametic Sphinx c.10,000 BCE to the present, which makes recorded history about 12,000 years old. Keep in mind, that as we have discussed what we know as western recorded history does not come onto the world stage until the around the time of Homer in the last millenium BCE.

It is the **last approximately 3,600** years that the **Afrikan worldview comes under notable attack.** History provides a reasonably clear record of approximately when the various worldviews immerged onto recorded history. History also clearly indicates which views were attacked, when and by whom. The Summary table, below lists the battle numbers, types and outcomes, as I understand them. Following the table you will find a summary of each of the battles.

Table 6 Ten Battles of the Cultural War

Bat. #	Date	Battle Name	Type of Battle	Outcomes
1	c.1675 B.C.E.	Hyksos invasion	Physical Battle 1	Afrikan Culture dominant
2	c.666 BCE	1st Classical Invasions	Physical Battles 2, 3	Afrikan culture dominant
3	332 BCE	2nd Classical Invasions	Physical Battles 4, 5	South East West Culture
4	600 ACE- Present	The Information Battle	*Psycho-info Battle 1*	1st attack on Af. Culture
5	1492-1947	The Modern invasions	Physical Battle 6	Spread of Anti-think
6	1920-1930	Afrikan Centered Battle	*Psycho-info Battle 2*	Cultural Resurrection
7	1947-1994	African Independence Battle	Leg. Pol. Econ. Battle 1	Antithink dominant
8	1950 60's- Present	Civil Rights Battle	Leg. Pol. Econ. Battle 2	Cultural Cold War
9	1960's-1980	Afro-centric Battle	*Psycho-info Battle 3*	Cultural Resurrection
10	1980-2000+	Cultural Literacy Battle	*Psycho-info Battle 4*	Cultural Reassertion

The table above summarizes the 12 major battles of the cultural Wars, some of which continue to this day, primarily between Africans, their American descendants and Europeans. Being that it is a summary, the table is not intended to be all-inclusive.

1. The Hyksos Invasion (1675 BCE[2])

The Hyksos Invasion of Kamit (Egypt) was the first time in recorded history, that individuals from outside of Afrika came into Afrika in any significant numbers. They were physically repulsed by the Afrikans, and their invasion had no effect on the over 3.5 million years of human cultural development and knowledge, represented in classical Afrikan high

---

[2] (Note: BCE = Before the Common Era. CE = Common Era.)

culture of that time. c1700 Hebrews enter Kamit. This ebb, and flow of people in Africa does not bring civilization to Africa. The visitors in point of fact learn from Afrikan culture (inventors of civilization) the nature, and scope of civilized urban life and adapt, modify and spread their new-found knowledge in the known world.

2. First Classical Invasions [3] (666 BCE)

The 10,000 year classical Afrikan civilization of Kamit ends in 666 BCE, with the invasion of the **Assyrians** (Syrians) followed by the **Persians** (Iranians) 550B.C.E.

3. Second Classical Invasion (332 BCE)

The next group of invaders to occupy the classical Afrikan high culture of Kamit, was the **Greeks** lead by Alexander the so-called "great" 332BCE. This was the first mostly White invasion of Africa. Then came the **Romans** in 30BCE and finally the Arabs (Islam) in c640-642 CE. The ancestors of the present occupiers of Kamit (Arabs who bear no resemblance to the pyramid builders) came into Kamit during the 6th and 7th century CE.

4. The Information Battle (600 Ce to present)

The first three battles were primarily physical, and had a beginning and an end. This is the first battle that is on going to this day. Rather than ending at a particular point in time, it runs in parallel with battles 5 through 12.

5. The Modern Invasions (1492 to 1947)

The Modern Invasions is the 5th battle. It starts with Europeans leaving the area of the world they lived in to invade, enslave, rob and pillage the land of others. In the Old World the focus was Afrika and Australia. In the New World the focus was the America's. The **unprovoked physical**

---

[3] Sources: African People in World History by John Henrik Clarke

attacks in this battle follow a **1-2 pattern**. First a group of "explorers" and/or Christian missionaries come and are received as friends in other lands. Secondly, larger groups of invaders attack the native inhabitants using advanced war technology including biological warfare, (Small Pox infected blankets) given to native Americans, and Zulu's in Afrika. This pattern of attack is typically described by doublespeak words like colonialism, settlement, or settlers. At the end of this battle, four of the five inhabited continents are completely over run and forcibly controlled by Europeans. That is military, economic, political, and attempted cultural control. Hundreds of millions of the four continent's inhabitants (people of color) lay dead.

6. African Centered Battle (1920-1930's)

This battle starts with Garvey, and the back to Afrika movement. Finally, after the War of Enslavement when the dust settles Afrikans are still standing, and the cries rise up from the earth, *Afrika for the Afrikans*!

As Dr. Clarke, and others have pointed out prior to the civil war and the Emancipation, Africans considered there forced association with America temporary, and did expect to return to their motherland. You should be aware especially our youth that Marcus Garvey did not so much start the "back to Africa" movement as he **reintroduced, popularized and internationalized a movement** that did always exist in the Afrikan community here in America. The banner of **African nationalism** that Garvey picked up, and popularized comes down to us as what is today referred to as **pan-Africanism**

7. African independence Battle (1947 to 1994)

Garveyism temporarily was stalled in America, but supercharged an African independence explosion on the African continent. Black Nationalism Fathered by Martin Delany carried forward by Garvey, and later reflected in the pan-African movement in Africa.

The **Berlin conference of 1884** started the formal carving up of the Afrikan continent by the White Anti-humanists of Europe. The invasions started on the coasts of Afrika and spread to the interior. By the early 1900's all of Afrika and Australia and the sub continent of India was invaded and occupied. This process was called colonialism. The successful battle strategies for defeating overt colonialism starts in the 1940's, and culminates with South Africans regaining political control of their country in the 90's

Note: colonialism is a doublespeak word for invasion, and wholesale murder, and resource theft.

8. The Civil Rights Battle (1950's 60's-Present)

The civil rights battle **in America was** fought in parallel, with the Afrikan Independence Battle fought on the continent. The Civil Rights Battle was and is **being fought on three fronts** Legal, Political, and Economic. African Americans launched three major offensives to overturn the forces of racism in specific American institutions (E.G. Equal education in public schools). The success of some of those battles led to the rising African American middle class of the 80's and 90's.

History has demonstrated that all three of these segments of American society had **impediments designed to limit African American full citizenship.** Anti-humanist forces impacted everything from the law to economic freedom. The fact that African American human, and civil rights were adversely impacted by these institutions made them battle targets.

9. The Afro Centric Battle (1960's to 1980's)

This is the "I'm Black and I'm proud movement" Unlike the "I am A Man" signs of Dr. King. I'm Black and I'm proud is a cultural statement rather then a civil rights statement. It comes more from the desegregationist's like the Black Panther self defense party, and the popular music of James Brown. It is that time in African American history when African

Americans move from a generally less positive image of them selves, to a more positive image (I am Black and I am proud). The difference between afrocentrism, and cultural literacy can be stated as follows. "I'm Black and I'm proud" versus I'm Black and "I'm proud and I know why!" The, "I know why" part, is the cultural literacy aspect of personal and group pride. It is the "I know why" aspect of this battle that leads us to the final battle we call cultural literacy.

10. The Cultural Literacy Battle (1980-2000 plus)

The Current Battle (1998 in America) I call this battle the "Cultural Literacy Battle", it consist of forces in two camps the *Out of Afrika* **and** *Not Out of Africa camps.* The current Out of Afrika Camp consists of a new breed of Afrikan scholars, and spiritual leaders who are resurrecting, reconstructing, and restoring Africa's contribution to the world. Arrayed against them are racist, Caucasian scholars, and other Cultural Terrorist. The school of thought they represent is called the orthodox school of western history. Like the people they write about they have been less then fair and forth coming with the truth. They have prevented African scholars from having full and free access to African information. Therefore, the scholastic playing field is not even. In fact, African Scholars are systematically excluded from important information, as attested to by scholars like Dr. Ben, and Dr. Van Sertima.

Despite the impediments thrown up by anti-humanists, Afrikan scholars, and spiritual leaders have made tremendous **progress in resurrecting the Afrikan story**. There is now a wealth of detailed, well-documented information available in bookstores around the nation, and increasingly more available on the Internet. Most importantly, recapturing the wisdom of the ancients will change the world in ways that can hardly be imagined today.

The cultural literacy battle is the final battle, and it is just starting. It is the battle that must bring all previous, and current battles to a positive end. It is a hand to hand, man to man, fight that will dominate the next century at minimum. It will be fought in the home, in the schools, in the workplace, and in cyberspace. It is a renewed battle for truth, through which America must finally find her moral compass, and set an example for the world from the high ground to which the compass leads.

Part II Summery

At the end of **PART II CULTURAL LITERACY** We looked at the RaceSpeak Model, the Afrikan Aunk, and the Cultural War. Part II provided insight into the big picture regarding Cultural Poisoning. It also introduced us to Classical African Civilization thinking, which is the bases for and location of, the beginning of the cultural war.

We have utilized Cultural Literacy Minutes to think about the broader implications of Cultural poisoning regarding global ethnic groups as mapped by the **RaceSpeak Model**. In 1998 some may have looked at the end of the model. I.e. New World Order, "Race" War or New Global Village, and thought is overly dramatic. The events of 9/11/01 make it even clearer that what we do and do not know about the cultures of others, we interact with can cost us dearly. Cultural Literacy is a serious business.

So now it seems that we are in the early stages of a global "terrorism" War, hmm!

Next, we took a look at Classical African Civilization's multi-purpose **Aunk**. We used the Aunk to introduce us to some of the concepts, and thinking of Classical Africans. Lastly, we Looked at the **Cultural War** and concluded that it is important to understand were the battlefield and which army you are fighting, with the Humanist or the Anti-humanist.

In the end, we came to understand that someone else can not make you Culturally Literate. An elder or this section of DoubleSpeak can point you in the right direction, but the tires hit the road when you begin to do your own research about your legacy.

The Cultural Literacy Movement is a leaderless movement. The good news is that unlike the Civil Rights Movement. CL will not be stopped by killing a leader, there is none. As Malcolm said each one teach one. As the African American ethnic group becomes Culturally Literate, no one will have to tell us to act in our own best interest. We will do so automatically.

Part III

"Race" in the Third Millenium

"Race" in The Third Millenium

What's Next?

THE ACTION PLAN

Ok so here we are in the Third Millenium, what's next? **The eradication of Cultural Poisoning is next**. That is we will eradicate CP in the U.S.A. and with it the American "race" Problem. To achieve this new millenium objective we need a plan. Cultural Literacy requires action to gain traction.

Now that you know what Cultural Literacy and Cultural Poisoning are, what are you going to do about it? We are going to use this knowledge to take ourselves off cultural defense, and put ourselves on offence. Then we will move our families off defense, and onto the offensive team. Then you and I will do the same for our community, and ethnic group. A Nation can only lead from the moral high ground. And so America must change its ways so it can finally stand up on that high ground.

And so I say to you in words not on like our Dr. Kings words. That I have been to the mountaintop, I've looked over and seen the promise land. I may not get there with you, but America will get to the promise land. The new Team America will take its place in the Global Village in a way not envisioned by many today.

On hearing this vision some will say, no way. But one should keep in mind that just yesterday few could see the South Africa of today, until the humanists had their way. Looking back on yesterday, one can see clearly that when the humanist in Azania (South Africa) go together the nation was changed over night. It Started with African New School (youth) and Old School (elders) getting together to form a new unity. And the rest is history.

And so it is here in America, in your time, that New School and Old School must get together. Forming a new unity to cause the humanist to once again reinvent America. We have transformed, re-engineered, and morphed this nation before, and we must do it again so she can stand on the moral high ground of world leadership with other nations like Mandela's Azania.

Dr. King's dream, that long-standing African dream, has not died. It has gotten some new tools, and once again stood up and dusted itself off, and is marching forward at home and abroad.

The third millenium will go down in history as the **African Cultural Revolutionary Millenium**. Many writers believe that the third millenium will be the Asian Millenium. I agree that it will start out that way. China is a huge market with more then a billion people. They well do well economically. However, Africans on the continent, and in the Diaspora also more then a billion people, will be the surprise of the millenium. As the humanist of the world rise up in the new global village there will be much more MAAT (balance) between the worlds major ethnic groups. I expect Team American to be leading the way

Now to get from here to there, we will need that plan. We call the plan **The Cultural Literacy Action Plan.** The Action Plan is in two parts. One part of the plan is geared to raising Cultural Literacy, and the other is focused on reducing Cultural Poisoning (CP).

1. Reading Action Plan
2. CP Attack Plan

The Reading Action Plan has two components **Current Events** and Cultural reading. Ok, you expected Cultural reading but what about this current events stuff? Our youth need to pay special attention here. To be an effective local, and global citizen one must keep up with what is going on around you. You have more choices today Print Media, TV/Radio, and the Internet. And more flexible access points. Cell Phones, PDA's other mobile devices. Use the way that works for you, but be sure to get the news everyday.

Cultural Reading, That is raising your Cultural Literacy on a regular bases. Read the Cultural Literacy Trilogy, and the Cultural Literacy Basic Reading List for a start. Weather you read a book a day, a book a week, or a book a month, you must set a reading goal, and then execute the plan. I recommend that you start with the Trilogy.

First let me refresh your memory regarding the cultural literacy trilogy. **The first book** is entitled **DoubleSpeak in Black and White, E-published in 1998, paperback in 2002.** I provided you with an overview of the cultural literacy project. The Cultural Poisoning self test was the main feature of this book. The primary focus of the book was shedding some light on cultural poisoning, and its antidote. This is **volume one** in the trilogy. In completing *Doublespeak In Black And White* you have just completed part one of the trilogy.

The second book in the trilogy is **African American Rites of Passage**. It is intended to be a road map to cultural literacy. That is it will not make you Culturally Literate but serve as a road map to the bases you will need to touch on your journey. It is scheduled for release in **2003**.

The third book is titled simply **2084** due out in the year **2005**. 2084 is a novel that demonstrates the potential effects of the cultural literacy strategy. It puts a new twist on the ideas presented in the classic book Orwell's 1984. It is two visions of the future. One vision demonstrates what the world could look like if we take the medicine, the other vision demonstrates what the world is likely to look like, if we fail to take the medicine. It challenges the reader to think about which vision he, or she will help create for the new millenium.

You can **find out more** about the Cultural Literacy Project and the availability of the 21st Century Trilogy by contacting the Cultural Literacy Project in cyberspace at:

Web Site Cultural Literacy Central URL http://nuuaunk.findhere.com
Visit a Cultural Literacy 101 Club at Delphi, Yahoo, MSN or your
favorite cyber-community
E-mailing me at raunk@iname.com

Now, let us look at the four **reading recommendations of the Action
Plan**. They can be thought of as a **cultural literacy BEGINNER'S BOOK
SET**. You should keep in mind that an action plan is not just collecting
information but changing behavior. To be effective, you must put the
information you receive into practical action that improves your ethnic,
and economic effectiveness. See the following list:

<u>First</u>, the most used book in every African American's library should be,
The African American Holiday of Kwanzaa subtitled *a Celebration of
Family, Community & Culture*. By Maulana Karenga

The Honorable Mr. Karenga has combined traditional African culture,
and contemporary African American culture, into a modern set of
Cultural values interests, and principles which all African Americans
would be well served by Adapting as **a moral minimum**. Whether, your
are Black or White this is an excellent introduction to contemporary
African American Values, Interests, and Principles (VIP).

<u>Second</u>, a history book that should be in everyone's library is **African
People in World history** by the honorable ancestor Dr. John Henrik
Clarke.

The book is less then a hundred pages, and very fast reading. Dr. Clarke
was one of our greatest African scholars and has done an outstanding job,
of setting forth African history in a short yet detailed and comprehensive
format.

<u>Third</u> is a very encompassing book entitled, **What They Never Told
You In History Class**. By Indus Khamit-Kush 1983.

This book touches on every thing from the origin of man, religion, and
medicine to African American astronauts. The book does what its title

says; tells you what most of us should have been taught in high school history class but were not.

Fourth a book for our youth entitled **The Little Black Book**. By Carol Taylor

This is a pocket book that **every Male youth of color in America should have** in his pocket. Among other things it tells our youth what to do, and why when confronted by the police. It is a small book (fits in your pocket) and only costs a few dollars. She can be reached at (718) 856-1271.

This book is so important that I have to say just a few words about it here. It is time for old-school (elders) African Americans, to circle the wagons, and protect our future. 75% of individuals being imprisoned now, are people of color according to experts in the field, like Jerome Miller. The incarceration rate for African American women has risen by 400%. African American New York Supreme Court Justice Bruce Wright, has been advising us for years regarding the rampant racism in the criminal justice system. Now Mr. Miller, a European American provides dramatic information that informs us that the situation is at a critical danger point. He cautions America in his new book Search and Destroy African Americans in the Criminal Justice System, that America is traveling down a slippery slope. There are 5.5 million African American males between 18-39 and 75% of them are projected to be involved in the criminal justice system.

If you have a son, a nephew, or simply young African American male friends get them this book. It just may save their life!

Note: 9/11/01 The Attack on American and its "patriot" act have not helped. An American can now be picked up, and put in jail on suspicion with no charges. This book is more important to more people then when I first recommended it.

As we come to the end of the Action Plan **there are two very important things you can do** which will make a difference in American life right now.

First continue our discussion. Get *African American Rites of Passage, Understanding Classical African Civilization.*

Second make the **Seven Point CP Attack** part of your plans to move onto the cultural offensive in the cultural war. See the Seven Point CP Attack on the next page. Use the plan every day. Put it up in the kitchen, or in your bedroom. Make a copy of it and give it to a friend, help get them on the African good foot.

Once again good luck on your journey

THE SEVEN POINT CP ATTACK

Moving from defense to offense: a personal action plan

1. Learn all you can about Cultural Poisoning (CP)

2. Make a cultural judgement about all words.
Determine if words, phrases and/or lines of thinking you hear or use, are parts of doublespeak.
That is, are they words that represent or misrepresent reality?

3. Erase cultural doublespeak programs from your biocomputer
Correct (realign with reality) all doublespeak words, phrases and lines of thinking that have poisoned your normal mental process.

4. Vaccinate your children against CP
Once you have become effective at managing CP in yourself, you are in a position to prevent your children from catching it.

Listen to our male youth, they are calling themselves the "N" word and calling their women the "B" word. What words are the young people you know using? Give them the offensive weapons essential to preventing this type of acute cultural poisoning.

5. Educate or Attack CP users
Do not allow your culture to be disrespected, misrepresented, or otherwise denigrated.

Educate, if the CP user is misguided, or simply mis-educated. Suffer no fools in this respect. Do not permit misguided cultural statements to go un-responded to, fix them when you hear them. Your action will reduce cultural poisoning, and this is good for the individual and humanity.

Attack, (verbally) if the CP user is a cultural terrorist (Creator of CP, not just a carrier).
The objective of an attack is to expose, or otherwise neutralize a cultural terrorist's capacity to infect others.

6. Move to the next level, Cultural Literacy
Gain a sound working knowledge of your culture, and the culture (s) of those you interact with. To understand African/African American culture start with Classical African Civilization.

7. Get back in the learning loop and find your ZOD
The Zone of Optimal Development (ZOD) is the time and space where you have acquired the capacity to optimize your spiritual, cultural, and economic effectiveness.

Cultural Literacy and Economic Literacy
For 21st Century Effectiveness

Hetep,
Rudy Aunk
Cultural Literacy Requires Action the gain traction.
raunk@iname.com

Part III Summery

We have come to the end of PART III "RACE" IN THE THIRD MILENIUM. What did we gain? We have a clear objective for the millenium, eradicate Cultural Poisoning. You now have an action plan for moving forward culturally, **The Cultural Literacy Action Plan.** That is you have some new millenium tools to help you reduce Cultural Poisoning, and Raise Cultural Literacy for yourself and others on an on going bases.

You have the Three-Part **Reading Action Plan**
1. Currents Events Reading Plan
2. The Cultural Literacy Trilogy
3. The Cultural Literacy Beginners book set

You have the **Cultural Poisoning Attack Plan**
- Seven activities that you can employ on an ongoing bases, that put you on the cultural offensive.
- Objective: eradicate CP in the U.S.A. and with it the American "race" Problem. Then utilize the moral high ground of American success to leverage the eradication Cultural Poisoning in the world, in this third millenium

CONCLUSION

Congratulations you have completed DoubleSpeak in Black and White. In a minute we will briefly review were we have been with regard to Cultural Poisoning, Cultural Literacy, and "Race' in the New Millenium. But first there is one final area of economic importance, I would like to place on your radar screen for consideration.

As we come to the close, I would be remiss if I did not say a brief word about **Computer Literacy**. By profession I am a computer technologist. I have spent more then 30 years in the technology business with some of the largest forward thinking firms in the world. This experience has made one thing painfully clear to me regarding African Americans. We as a group were unwilling participants in the agricultural revolution in this country. We were for the most part left out of the Industrial Revolution. We can not afford to miss the Information Revolution.

Whether you are Black or White, **A Doctor, Lawyer, or A Native American Chief** you need to become effective at utilizing Information Technology (Computers). As I have traveled around the country many have said to me things like I don't have a need for a computer, or I can't afford to join the computer revolution. I would say this to you, "there are **three kinds of people in the world**, those who make things happen, those who things happen to, and those who wonder what happened." For your own economic will being it is imperative that you do not wake up in the middle of the Information Revolution wondering what happened. In fact, for African Americans I would say the **imperative for the next century** is Cultural Literacy, and Economic Literacy. One is good for the spirit, and the other for the pocket book. As someone once said to me, it is important to remember to eat while you feed your spirit. With respect to Economic

Literacy, I advocate Computer Literacy as an indispensable competency target regardless of what your means of earning a living might be today, a computer will be part of your work tomorrow. I will stop on that note. Suffice it to say here that **information** and what you do with it **has a major role both in cultural and economic literacy.**

What you understand and believe about how much you can earn often determines what you earn in reality. And so it is with respect to culture, what you believe your culture is, is in reality what your culture is.

I have been asking you to **think about what you believe regarding ethnicity and culture.** The self made millionaire Anthony Robins of TV self-help fame often points out that beliefs determine reality. In his book Unlimited Power, he cites the case of a remarkable study on schizophrenia. A woman with normal blood sugar, when she believed she was diabetic, her belief became her reality (Her blood sugar changed to that of a diabetic). **What you believe about ethnicity and culture is America's reality.** If South Africa can change their reality then we can create a new harmony in Team America.

Finally, the **specter of Doublespeak and** cultural poisoning, is an ominous information force that has disrupted the natural ebb, and flow of human kind for the last two millenniums. As we move further into the information age it is imperative that the cultural poisoning does not move with us.

We have looked at a considerable amount of information that can help Americans eradicate cultural poisoning in the next millenium. **In the PREFACE** we made the assertion that the road to finally resolving America's "race" problem starts with language.

In PART I CULTURAL POISONING we then went on to provide **two graphic models**, one that outlined the problem, and one that outlined the solution process. And the answers to the Cultural Poisoning Self-Test were provided.

The first model is the cultural literacy projects conceptual "problem analysis model" (The American "race" problem model). The model points to two specific problems that are among America's most visible, remarkable and intractable problems, American disharmony, and African American disunity. We have proposed a new definition for the bottom line cause of both of these problems, Cultural Poisoning. The **second model** (the Cultural Literacy Strategy) which outlines our proposed solution, describes the components of the problem, and solution process. It starts with culturally infected people, and ends with cured people operating in a psychosocial place of maximum wellbeing we call the ZOD.

The balance of the information presented in **PART I** was designed to take us from the **conceptual model framework, to practical examples** of cultural poisoning on the ground, in the nation and in individuals. Each example (Answer to the **10 Questions**) endeavored to point out two things. First the specific information deficiency which we called a cultural virus for example, geographic AIDS. Second each example provided an antidote (reality based cultural information) which leads to reduced Cultural Poisoning, and increased Cultural Literacy (cultural health). Last we looked at 2 questions beyond the ten.

America's complex intractable **"race" problem is not unsolvable.** The answer has been staring Western society in the face since the time of Orwell's 1984. Language represents the thoughts that make up our social reality. Therefore, if we **change our language** and by default our thoughts, we will change America's social reality. History has demonstrated that to do otherwise simply produces patches and/or partial solutions, and leaves America with open wounds.

In PART II CULTURAL LITERACY we utilized Cultural Literacy Minutes to think about the broader implications of Cultural poisoning regarding global ethnic groups as mapped by the RaceSpeak Model. We took a look at Classical African Civilization's multi-purpose Aunk. Lastly we Looked at the Cultural War and concluded that it is important to understand were the battlefield is and who's side we are on.

In the end, we came to understand that someone else can not make you Culturally Literate, you must do the heavy lifting yourself.

The Cultural Literacy Movement is a leaderless movement. It is a movement that requires that you lead yourself guided by your Great Spirit, and the honorable ancestors, who have paid much for you to stand here today. It requires only your good will, and the personal actions necessary to manifest that will.

The last part of the book **PART III "RACE" IN THE THIRD MILLENIUM**

We set the cultural objective for the new millenium; eradicate Cultural Poisoning! We said we needed a plan and we recommended a Reading Plan, and the CP Attack Plan, to achieve our objective.

Finally, the race problem is not a conceptual conflict between that European American ethnic group, and that African American ethnic group, over there. (Substitute any American groups) It is a conflict between **you and me** sitting across the table from each other, at the national discussion on "race". The fix starts with you and me examining our language, thoughts, and behaviors. Are they positive, neutral, or negative regarding forming a new harmonious Team America? What is necessary in the end, is not just thinking, but a quantum change in national behavior, driven by individuals. What we need is a behavior change by individuals who have recalibrated their moral behavioral compasses to point in the humanist direction rather than in the opposite direction.

Any American of good will that is interested in seeing America and his ethnic group continue to progress into the next century should be interested in dismantling cultural poisoning. At a minimum, you should be interested in minimizing the personal effects of it on yourself and your children. As I stated before man's first civilization coined the phrase **MAN KNOW THY SELF**. Debriefing yourself with respect to cultural poisoning is a major part of getting to know yourself. And now that you have gotten started, you're on your way to the ZOD. Good Luck!

You must fight and defeat the evil within or you will pass it on to your children as surely as your parents passed it on to you

About the Author

Rudy Aunk is a techno-cultural activist, author, and founder of the Cultural Literacy Project. He has successfully combined his dual passions for computers and culture, into concrete tools that can help individuals regain, and/or maintain, cultural health. In Cyberspace he is simply known as Aunk (Ankh).

Rudy is pictured here in his former role, as Director of Information Technology, and Chief Technologist at the National Urban League. Currently you can find Aunk in CyberSpace, still stretching the technology, and hosting what he likes to call his worldwide radio show (Cultural Literacy 101 audio chat). Visit the Projects web site, Cultural Literacy

Central for dates, times, and places. If you are on-line, stop by, up close and personal, and get a cultural check up from the neck up.

http://come.to/aunk

NOTES AND BIBLIOGRAPHY

1. [i] Ancient Egyptian Proverbs. Compiled, By Dr. Muata Ashby.

[ii] Those of you, who are having a brain crash, and descending into **footnote foolishness** (it's not true if there is no footnote), think for yourself for a minute. You don't actually need a footnote pointing to a thorough study complete with irrefutable statistics to understand this reality. All you need to do is read American history and avoid forgetting the bad parts.

[iii] Also called the parental AIDS test. You will learn what AIDS means in this context, in the next section

[iv] Man God and Civilization, By John G. Jackson.

[v] Two Nations, Black and White. Separate, Hostile, Unequal, By Andrew Hacker. (New York Times Bestseller).

[vi] African Americans who have not heard the words cultural literacy, should understand that it is not a new concept. Using it as a popular phrase related to African Americans may be relatively new, but not the concept. Most ethnic and/or national groups formally teach their adults and children to be literate in their culture. Examples of cultures are European (ethnic) and American (national). In fact there is a national bestseller called Cultural Literacy, What Every American Needs to Know, By E.D. Hirsch, JR.

[vii] The New Doublespeak, Why No One Knows What Anyone's Saying Anymore, By William Lutz. P27-32 There is a theory of how language affects the way we see the world. Edward Sapir first expressed this theory in the west in 1929. Later it became known as the Sapir-Whorf theory, still later this became the Whorf theory. In 1940, Whorf

argued that each language conveys to its users a ready-made worldview. Whorf made the following statement that is critical to understanding African American unity and American Harmony. In talking about his new linguistic theory of relativity he says the following. "All observers are not led by the same physical evidence to the same picture of the universe. Unless their linguistic backgrounds are similar, or can in some way be calibrated" equally important Lutz goes on to say" that it is not that language determines what we can think, but that language influences what we routinely think".

viii The Penguin Atlas of African History, By Colin McEvedy p8.

ix Including Dr. Ben, Dr. Clarke, Dr Van Sertimer, and Dr. Leonard Jeffries.

x Egypt revisited, By Ivan Van Sertima.

xi Black Athena, The Afroasiatic Roots of Classical Civilization. Volume 1: The Fabrication of Ancient Greece 1785-1985, By Martin Bernal.

xii The little "c." means approximate date and B.C.E. means before the Common Era. It is used in conjunction with C.E., meaning the Common Era. This convention is preferable to the BC AD Christian era convention as it tends to minimize the cultural poisoning effects of certain religious propaganda uses of BC AD.

2. xiii Egypt Child of Africa and Egypt Revisited, Edited, By Ivan Van Sertima. (The pyramid builders were Africans, plenty of proof, and footnotes from many different scholars).

xiv Black Indians, A Hidden Heritage By William Loren Katz. P29.

xv Bureau of Indian Affairs, U.S. Dept. of the Interior (1990 Census).

xvi From the Speech given by the senator from Hawaii at the United (Native American organization) sponsored National Native American youth conference carried on cable in July 1998.

xvii 1455 the papal Bull authorized European anti-humanists to "reduce to servitude all infidel people". Infidel defined as non-Christians (people without souls or without saved souls) like Africans and Native Americans. Christians were in effect morally authorized to commit any crime against humanity in the pursuit of "saving souls" and converting "heathens" to Christianity.

3. [xviii] From the Browder File, By Anthony T. Browder. p. 61 The Jesus ship information and in 1411 C.E. Portuguese enslavers brought the first enslaved Africans to the Pope. He deemed them to be "soulless people". The church invented something called "Divine Providence" to sanction and give religious cover to European enslavers.

[xix] The African Presence in Ancient America, They Came Before Columbus, By Ivan Van Sertima.

America B.C. Ancient Settlers in the New World, By Harvard Professor Barry Fell.

[xx] We Hold These Truths, Understanding the Ideas and the Ideals of the Constitution, By Mortimer J. Adler, p6.

[xxi] African People and European Holidays: Mental Genocide, By Rev. Ishakamusa Barashango. book two p121.

[xxii] ibid., p125.

[xxiii] ibid., p124.

[xxiv] ibid., p123.

4. [xxv] The confederate flag is a symbol of an American war in which the confederates fought to keep Africans in enslavement. This flag can still be found proudly hanging in governmental institutions. This is an insult in the same way naming a sports team the Red Skins, and having a Native American painted red as a symbol or mascot, is an insult to Native Americans. This is not the behavior of anyone who would call them selves a humanist. An American who was fighting for the right to enslave, and murder other human beings does not qualify as an American hero. If you don't think that anything is wrong with having confederates as American heroes, you are exhibiting a symptom of cultural poisoning. Fighting is not the sole criteria for measuring

heroism. It is what the person, or people are fighting for that determines whether their actions are meritorious.

xxvi The King James Version of the Holy Bible Revelation 1.14 one must take note that this passage reads differently in different flavors of the KJV. Different groups have put their own spin on different sections of the bible and approached the interpretation of the bible differently. For example, there is the American Bible Society flavor, the Good news bible, The Revised Standard Version, and many, many, more,

xxvii Stolen Legacy, By G.M. James.

xxviii The Story of Civilization, By Will Durant also see, What they never told you in history class, By Indus Khamit-Kush.

xxix The Washington Post May 4, 1979.

xxx What They Never Told You in History Class, By Indus Khamit-Kush There is a lot of information on this subject especially see, Dr. Ben and John G. Jackson.

xxxi Egypt Revisited, By Ivan Van Sertima P9.

xxxii See the writings of ancient historians like Herodotus, Strabo, Diodorus etc.

xxxiii African Origins of the Major World Religions, By Dr. Yosef Ben-Jochannan, Charles Finch, Modupe Oduyoye, Tsegaye Gabre-Medhin.

xxxiv Sex and Race Vol. 1 J.A. Rogers.

xxxv 7/1998 Cable documentary on Micheal Angelo and the Sistine Chapel paintings, CH 13.

5. xxxvi Metu Neter, Vol. 1 and 2, By Ra Un Nefer Amen.

6. xxxvii Egyptian YOGA, The Philosophy of Enlightenment, By Muata Ashby.

xxxviii Two Nations, Black and White. Separate, Hostile, Unequal, By Andrew Hacker. (New York Times Bestseller).

xxxix An Afrocentric Guide to Spiritual Union, By Ra Un Nefer Amen. The Power, Passion, and Pain of Black Love. By Jawanza Kunjufu. The average African divorce rate is commonly given as 5%. Some estimates go as high as 10%. The absolute figure is less important then the relations ship to western 50-80% figures.

[xl] Melanin: The Chemical Key to Black Greatness, By Mr. Carol Barnes.

[xli] When I use the term mixed, I am typically referring to human biological mixtures of a dominant gene group like Africans with a recessive gene group like Caucasians. For example, if an African melanated person mates with a Caucasian, the resulting biologically mixed offspring will typically have the same or less visible melanin than the African parent, but more visible melanin then the less melanated parent. Naturally there are exceptions, and ethnic groups other than the ones mentioned can produce biologically mixed offspring. I am here referring to multi-ethnic people in the general sense as a derived biological group.

[xlii] African Origin of Biological Psychiatry, By Richard King, M.D. p115.

0-595-22858-5